W9-CXX-594

Do-It-Yourself Decorating
Step-by-Step
Decorative Details

Jenny Plucknett

Meredith® Books
Des Moines, Iowa

Contents

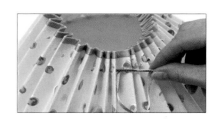

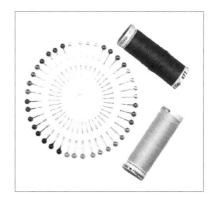

Very easy

A little skill

Some experience

Before You Begin

Creating successful soft furnishings relies in part on choosing the right fabrics and trimmings. This chapter outlines the most important factors to consider when shopping for fabrics, including tips on the effective use of color and pattern to carry out the look you have in mind and advice on selecting an appropriate weight and type of fabric. We also explain practical considerations, such as how to work out the quantities of material that you need and how to match the designs of patterned fabrics perfectly across widths.

This chapter introduces the basic materials used for the projects—fabrics, interlinings, and trimmings—and gives all the information necessary to choose the right products for each item you make.

Style and color

Understand the basic principles of style and color, as illustrated here, and you can make the most of a room of virtually any size or shape. In fact, with a little decorative sleight-of-hand you can "raise" a low ceiling or "expand" a tiny space.

IMPROVING ON A ROOM'S NATURAL POSITION AND SHAPE

▲ Cool down overly bright, sunny rooms with light blues or restful greens.

▲ Warm up and brighten cold rooms that receive little sunlight with sunny, stimulating colors such as yellow, orange, and red.

◀ Cozy up large rooms with bright colors and bold patterns. It still is wise to balance large designs with smaller coordinating patterns, checks, stripes, or plain colors.

◄ Overly high ceilings appear lower if they are clad in dark colors. Dark flooring and furniture also bring floor and ceiling together. Horizontal stripes on window treatments (and upholstered furniture, too) also lower the apparent height of the room.

▲ Pale tones on walls, ceiling, and floors make small rooms look more spacious. Soften colors where necessary by introducing a light-colored rug or wall hanging. Use floor-length curtains or blinds that match the wall color for an illusion of height.

► Low ceilings will seem higher if you carry your eye upward with vertical stripes on the walls and window treatments.

EFFECTIVE USE OF COLOR

Next time it rains while the sun is shining, study the colors in a rainbow—how they follow and blend into each other. By joining the ends of the rainbow to make a circle, the color wheel is formed, and this is used as the basis for color planning. The simplest scheme uses just one color, but in many shades. This is known as a monochromatic scheme. Adjoining colors are known as closely related colors and work well together. Look at the colors on the color wheel that lie on each side of the main color used in the room and pick these for a subtle addition. The complementary color is the color that lies directly opposite on the color wheel. It creates the strongest possible contrast. A complementary color should be used in small quantities and is ideal for accessories, borders, and piping, or for decorations, such as bows and flowers.

Choosing fabrics

We are almost always drawn to a fabric by its color and design. However, before making final decisions, there are other points to consider. What is the fabric made of? Can it be washed or must it be dry-cleaned? Is it tough enough to do the job it is intended to do, and how durable is it? And finally, will it look good in the location for which it is intended?

KNOWING YOUR FIBERS

If you know the fibers that are included in a fabric and the advantages and disadvantages of each, you'll be better prepared to choose the best fabric for the project.

Fabrics may be produced from natural or man-made fibers, or a mix of both. Natural fibers include cotton, linen, silk, and wool. These fibers are resistant to dust and dirt and clean well, although some may shrink when washed. Linen and silk wrinkle easily. Man-made fibers may be totally synthetic, such as polyester, nylon, and acrylics. They generally are easy to wash, wrinkle- and shrink-resistant, and tough. However, they attract dust and dirt and need regular cleaning. Man-made fibers often are mixed with natural fibers, creating a fabric with the benefits of each. Some man-made fibers, such as rayon, come from plant material that is chemically treated. This type of fiber has many of the features of totally synthetic fibers, but it is not as tough.

CHECKING FABRIC SUITABILITY

Before buying a fabric, be sure it is suitable for the job you want it to do. Fabrics fall into one of three categories. Most are light wear and suitable for curtains, cushions, and tablecloths. Tougher, close-woven fabrics work well for coverlets. Only heavy-duty fabrics are suitable for the hard wear that upholstery receives.

If you select a fabric with a large design, you will need to match the pattern repeat. You also may need to center the design, particularly on items such as cushions. Always check the size of the pattern repeat before making a purchase. Matching fabrics with bold motifs sometimes requires considerable amounts of extra fabric, making them an expensive choice.

When making table linens and other items that require frequent washing, make sure the fabrics are simple to launder.

Wrinkle a corner of the fabric in your hand, then release it to check whether the creases fall out or the fabric remains crumpled.

Thick fabrics are difficult to sew. Avoid them if you are making something that includes piping in the seams.

BUYING CHECKLIST

It is a good idea to make a few simple checks in the fabric store before buying the fabric. Most fabrics carry labels with information on fiber content, recommended uses, and cleaning instructions. If any information you need is not listed, ask a salesperson for assistance.

- Check color compatibility against carpet, paint, and fabric samples from the room.
- If a fabric has not been preshrunk and is likely to shrink, buy a 12-inch length to do a shrink test.
- Look for flame-resistant fabrics when covering upholstered furniture and sewing items for a child's room.
- Choose fabrics with stain-resistant finishes for furnishings that are not convenient to wash regularly.
- Check the length of fabric for flaws.
- Make sure the pattern is printed on the straight grain of the fabric.

HOME CHECKS

Once you've found a suitable fabric, purchase a sample and place it in the room where you plan to use it. Check the fabric's overall effect in the room. Also, look at it by day and night light, since colors appear quite different under artificial light. This extra effort early on may help avoid an expensive mistake in the long run.

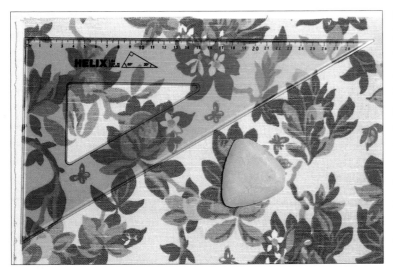

PREPARING FABRIC

Before cutting out your fabric, press it, then check the top edge to make sure it is cut straight with the grain of the fabric. Lay the fabric on a flat surface and place a triangle or other square-cornered object, such as a book, on the top edge to get a right angle. Extend the top edge of the right angle with a yardstick and draw a line along the fabric with tailor's chalk. Cut along the top edge following the drawn line and remove selvages down either side.

Using patterned fabrics

Introducing pattern in soft furnishings adds character and sparkle to a room scheme. Choose the main fabric first, and you have the basis for an easy-to-create room scheme. Mixing patterns is easy with so many coordinating fabrics available. However, careful planning is necessary to determine how and where to use each design. Once the fabrics are chosen, you need to work out the best arrangement of the design and the quantities of fabric required. A patterned fabric, matched accurately across the widths, hides seam lines in a way that is impossible on a plain one.

PLANNING A ROOM SCHEME

◀ If you are starting from scratch, one of the easiest and most effective ways of planning a scheme is to choose a fabric and use it as the basis for the scheme.

◀ The way a room is used affects the choice of patterns. Bold designs and bright colors are welcoming and are ideal for bathrooms and in open areas, such as a hall or stairway. For rooms where you spend more time, such as bedrooms or living rooms, choose a more relaxing background.

▲ The fabric design you choose can change the apparent shape of a room. Bold designs such as this one make an area appear smaller, while small designs increase the spacious look.

◄ Utilize coordinating patterns to create an integrated scheme. For your own pattern mix, pick a color, then choose florals, stripes, and checks based on it.

◄ Choose vertical stripes, as shown here, if you want to add height. Use horizontal stripes if you want to add width or length.

PATTERN REPEAT

◄ When buying fabric with bold designs, you need to establish how much extra fabric will be required to position the design in the best way possible and to match it across fabric widths. Check the length of the pattern repeat. On curtains, the lower edge of the design should be on the hem edge. For a tablecloth, wall hanging, or mat, the design is best centered. On a chair, the design needs to be centered on the outer chair back, inner chair back, seat cushions, and front edge, plus matched on inside and outside arms.

BUYING AND USING PATTERNED FABRIC

To estimate fabric quantities accurately, cut out paper pattern pieces for all the sections. Mark out an area on the table or floor that is the fabric's width and divide this into pattern repeat lengths. Arrange the pattern pieces within this area, checking that these are centered on the design or are mirror images where necessary. When satisfied with the arrangement, measure the length covered by the pattern pieces to get the quantity of fabric required. Remember to allow for the fact that the starting point on the fabric length could be at any point in the design.

When joining lengths of patterned fabric, the design needs to follow through on all the widths. The best way to make sure the match is accurate is to join widths using the ladder stitch (see page 78). Done from the right side of the fabric, this stitch ensures an accurate match. When the fabric is turned to the wrong side, a line of tacks is visible, ready for the seams to be machine-stitched.

Interfacings and linings

Some soft furnishings need stiffness and support, others need extra thickness, insulation, added softness, or weight. There is a range of specially produced materials to create whichever result you require. Most come in both dark and pale shades. Choose pale alternatives to go under light-colored fabrics and deeper shades under dark-colored fabrics.

INTERFACINGS AND INTERLININGS

Interfacings

These are attached to the wrong side of the main fabric to provide stiffness, shape, and support and usually are hidden by a lining. Match the interfacing in weight and laundering instructions to the main fabric.

Both sew-in or iron-on varieties of interfacing are available in a wide range of weights. Sew-in interfacings are more time-consuming to apply but, because they allow some movement, create a more natural result. They can be used to add body to fabrics, such as plastic laminates and metallics, which could be ruined by the use of a hot iron.

Interfacings may be woven or nonwoven. The nonwoven material usually is firmer than the woven alternative and does not fray. Woven interfacings, which contain some stretch, are ideal for use with fabrics that are cut on the bias.

Interlinings

Placed between the main fabric and the lining, interlinings add insulation, thickness, weight, and durability to home furnishings. Available in wide widths, they are ideal for use with larger items such as curtains, valances, and even tablecloths. One common interlining used for full-length draperies is a 100-percent-cotton flannel that has nap on both sides. Another interlining fabric that works well for items made of light- and medium-weight fabrics is a 100-percent cotton, loosely woven even-weave fabric. There also are interlinings of various fiber blends available for use as interlining materials. When in doubt, ask fabric-store personnel to guide you.

APPLYING INTERFACINGS

Sew-in interfacings

Lightweight to medium-weight interfacings can be stitched in the seam. Simply baste the interfacing to the wrong side of the fabric and sew as usual. Firm and heavyweight interfacings are sewn inside the seam lines. To do this, cut out the interfacing to match the fabric, then trim off the seam allowance. Place on the wrong side of the fabric, with outer edges just inside the seam lines. Tack in place, then herringbone-stitch the interlining in position. Sew as usual.

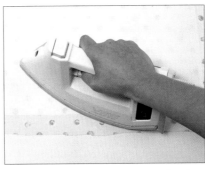

Iron-on interfacings

Lightweight iron-on interfacings can be stitched into the seam, but interfacings of a heavier weight should be cut to fit just inside the seam lines.

To affix, place the interfacing, adhesive side down, on the wrong side of the fabric. Cover with a damp cloth and, using a dry iron on a warm setting, press for about 15 seconds, one area at a time. Do not slide the iron across the fabric. Allow to cool. For heavier fabrics, turn the fabric over and press again on the right side.

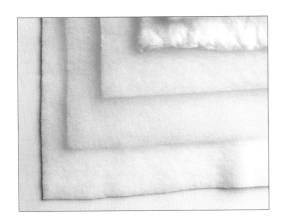

BATTINGS

Battings, which add bulk and insulation, come in both natural and man-made fibers. Cotton batting has a layer of fluffy material sandwiched between thin layers of cotton fabric. Use it with silk and other fine fabrics when hand quilting. Cotton batting must be hand-washed or dry-cleaned. Polyester batting is washable. It comes in a number of weights. The most common are: low-loft for use in appliqué, medium-loft for quilting, and high-loft for use in bed quilts and coverlets. Polyester batting also can be used to stuff small items, such as pillows.

LININGS

A lining not only neatens the wrong side, it also provides form and body and protects the main fabric from light and dirt. Choose the best lining that you can afford, since a poor-quality lining will wear out long before the main fabric. Cotton sateen is a widely used lining fabric. It comes in 48-inch and 54-inch widths and in a wide range of colors, including white and neutrals. Both easy-care polyester/cotton and wide-width cotton poplin also can be used as linings.

Trimmings and Tiebacks

Handmade trimmings, such as piping, ruffles, braids, and bows, are not difficult to produce, yet they add the finishing touch that turns a plain home furnishing into an exciting design that is unique to you. The effect trimmings create depends on their color, shape, and where you place them. They can be used to match a furnishing scheme, coordinate with it, or add a dramatic contrast.

These trimmings are easy to add to ready-made furnishings, too, and dress up simple shapes with a quick ruffle, bow, or a bold braided edge.

All of the trimmings featured in this chapter have an extra bonus. They can be added to or used to create curtain tiebacks for practical, attractive decorations in your home.

Trimming styles

Tiebacks decoratively hold curtains away from the window. To create the effect you want, you'll need to decide the position of the tiebacks in relation to the shape of the window, the drape of the fabric, and the length of the curtain. For instance, do you want to use tiebacks to highlight the curtain treatment? To show off a pretty window? Reveal a beautiful view? Let in or exclude light? All of these factors affect the position of the tiebacks. Before making a decision, cut a strip of fabric or string and hold it at various levels around the curtains to test the different effects and determine the final placement.

Each of the trimmings in this chapter can be used to embellish and add individuality to home furnishings.

TIEBACK CHOICES

◄ For a neat and subtle border to seams or edges, traditional smooth piping is effective. Try ruched piping for a more unusual finish. It's easy to do and decorative.

◄ Use a generous single bow to highlight a pretty pleat or flounce. To accentuate a shaped edge, add a line of small bows.

TIEBACK POSITIONS

▲ A tieback traditionally is positioned about two-thirds down a curtain's length. This low placement of the tieback allows the curtains to remain pulled across the window at the top edge and is ideal if you want to show off a curtain fabric or rich draping.

► Instead of pairing curtains, tie a single panel to one side for stunning impact. This covers much of the window, so it is not the best option if you want to show off ornate woodwork or a beautiful view, or if you have a dark room that needs maximum sunlight.

ATTACHING TIEBACKS

The simplest way to attach a tieback to a wall or window frame is to use a screw hook. Many attractive designs are available. To fix the hook into wood, start a small hole in the wood using a nail and hammer. Remove the nail, then screw in the hook. When screwing the hook into the wall, it is important to use a plastic wall plug. First drill a hole, tap in the wall plug until the end is flush with the wall, then screw the hook into the center.

▲ For a small or short window, consider placing tiebacks one-third of the way down full-length curtains or two-thirds the way down sill-length curtains. This allows the maximum amount of light into the room, as does hanging curtains as far to each side of the window as possible.

◄ The third choice for a full-length curtain is to place the tiebacks half-way down the curtain or at sill level, if the window is short. This shows off balanced swirls of fabric above and below the tieback.

CHECKING THE SIZE

Once you have decided on the tieback position, lightly mark the spot for the screw hook on the wall and hold a tape measure around the curtain at this point. Make sure the measurement allows for the amount of drape you want. Adjust if necessary, then note the length on the tape. This measurement is the length of your finished tieback.

Smooth piping

Piping is the traditional method for creating a neat, classic finish to an edge or seam on many soft furnishings. Use piping to crisply outline cushions and tiebacks, highlight chair and sofa seams, edge valances, curtains, and blinds, or divide colors on furnishing fabrics, ruffles, and pleats.

To form a smooth, rounded edge, piping cord is sandwiched within the piping fabric. Where a flat finish is required, fabric alone can be used without the addition of piping cord.

MATERIALS:
Furnishing fabrics, piping cord, matching thread, tailor's chalk
Plus for tiebacks: Heavyweight interfacing

FABRIC:
For piping: Measure all the seam lines and edges to be piped and add these measurements together. Include an additional 2 inches for each "join" (see box on joining piping, opposite) to give the total length of fabric strips and piping cord required. Allow for shrinkage when using cotton piping cord; wash before using. Fabric used for piping is cut on the bias in strips that are 2 inches wide (see below). *For tiebacks:* Draw the pattern to your required size (see page 91). You will need two pieces of fabric this size (or one of fabric and one of lining), one piece of interfacing, and two 18-inch lengths of 1-inch-wide ribbon for ties (or, make ties from 3-inch-wide lengths of piping fabric).

MAKING PIPING

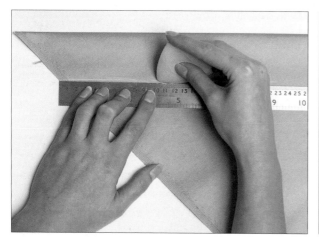

1 To cut out bias strips, fold the fabric at a 45-degree angle. To do this, lay the fabric flat with selvages to the right and left. Take one of the top corners and fold it diagonally to the opposite selvage. Press the fold, then draw in parallel lines on the fabric at 2-inch intervals with a piece of tailor's chalk. Cut out the strips.

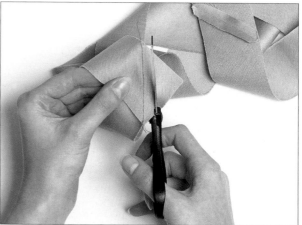

2 Join strips of fabric to make up the length of piping required. Pin pieces together with right sides facing, then machine-stitch together with narrow seams along the straight grain of the fabric. Trim the seams, then press them open. Fold the fabric strip in half lengthwise with wrong sides facing and matching the raw edges.

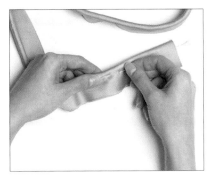

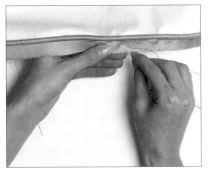

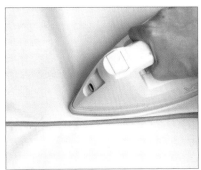

3 Encase the piping cord inside the folded strip and pin in place. Using a zipper foot, stitch along the strip close to the cord. Begin stitching ½ inch from one end and stop 2 inches from other end to allow for joining piping.

4 Place the stitched line of the covered piping strip along the seam line on one piece of fabric to be piped with right sides facing and raw edges even. Pin piping to the fabric, then stitch in place.

5 With right sides facing and raw edges even, position the second piece of fabric over the stitching line of the piping. Baste in place along the seam line. Stitch, turn fabric to the right side, and press.

JOINING PIPING ENDS TOGETHER

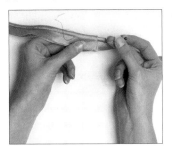

Stop stitching 2 inches before ends of the piping meet up. Trim the cord to meet exactly, but allow an overlap of ½ inch of fabric beyond the join. Turn fabric under ¼ inch and enclose the raw fabric end at the start of the piping. Continue stitching across the join.

PIPED TIEBACK

1 Using Pattern A on page 91, cut out a piece of interfacing to the size of the finished tieback and two pieces of fabric to the tieback size (the pattern includes ½-inch seam allowances all around). Place the interfacing, centered, on the wrong side of front tieback shape. Use herringbone stitch (see page 79) to attach interfacing to fabric.

2 Make enough piping to go around tieback, following steps 1–3, Making Piping. Stitch piping to the right side of interfaced tieback shape following Step 4. Press under seam allowance on the second fabric piece, snipping into the allowance so it lies flat; pin in place, attaching one end of each ribbon tie between the shapes, as shown. Slip-stitch the lining in place, covering the raw edges.

Ruched piping

Ruched piping is made in a similar way to smooth piping, but the strip is gathered to create the ruched finish. Use thick piping cord to create a dramatic effect.

Lightweight to medium-weight fabrics that gather well are most suitable for ruched piping; however, piping fabric needs to be of a similar weight to the main fabric. Mix plain piping with patterned fabric and vice versa to create the strongest impact.

MATERIALS:
Lightweight to medium-weight fabric, piping cord, matching thread
Plus for tiebacks: Soft rope or extra-thick cord, two curtain rings

FABRIC:
For piping: To calculate the length of fabric required, measure all seam lines and edges to be piped. Add measurements together, then double the final figure. Include an additional 2 inches for each join. For piping cord, use the single measurement around seams and edges. Allow for shrinkage when using cotton piping cord and wash before using. Cut fabric for ruched piping into 2½-inch-wide bias strips (see page 18).
For tiebacks: To calculate the fabric required, measure the finished length for each tieback (see page 17). Double this length, then add 1 inch (for turn-under allowances at the ends). For the width, measure around the rope or cord used and add 2 inches to this measurement. For each tieback you also will need four circles of fabric twice the diameter of the cord end.

MAKING RUCHED PIPING

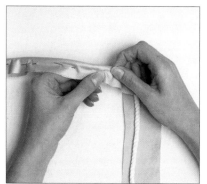

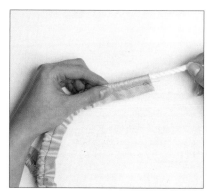

1 Make up the length of fabric required from bias strips (see steps 1 and 2, page 18). Fold the fabric in half lengthwise with the wrong sides facing and matching the raw edges. Place the end of the piping cord at one end of the fabric strip; encase it in the fabric. Pin along the edge to secure.

2 Using large machine stitches, baste across the end of the cord and fabric to hold them in place. Allowing a small space between cord and stitching line, stitch for about 8 inches. Stop and gently pull the cord through the fabric to create gathers. Evenly adjust the gathers.

3 Hold the cord taut and continue stitching and gathering until the cord end is reached. Add extra bias strips, if necessary. When the gathering is as full as you want it, baste across the cord end with large machine stitches, temporarily holding the cord in place.

RUCHED TIEBACK

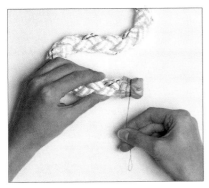

1 Cut out one fabric strip for each tieback to the required length (see Fabric, page 20). Fold strip in half lengthwise with right sides facing. Stitch the long edge, making a fabric tube. Turn the tube right side out. For each rope end, baste two fabric circles together and place over the end. Stitch the circles around the sides of the rope to secure (you cannot attach to the sealed rope ends), then wind thread around the fabric-encased rope end. Pull the rope through the fabric tube and fold under the seam allowance at each end. Run a gathering stitch in each fold.

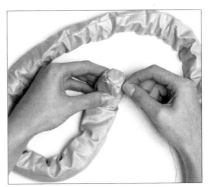

2 Pull up the gathering threads, fitting the ends of the fabric tube to the rope ends, then stitch together as shown here. Adjust fabric gathers so that they are even along the length of the tieback. Attach a ring to the tieback at each end, overstitching the ring to the fabric-covered rope end to hold it in place.

4 Adjust gathering if necessary so that it is even along the length, then attach piping to one main fabric piece (see Step 4, page 19). Once attached, unpick threads across the piping cord and join ends of piping together (see Joining Piping Ends Together, page 19).

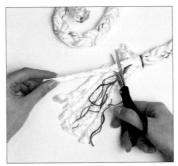

PREPARING NYLON ROPE

Thick, soft nylon rope ravels quite easily. Ask the shop to cut the lengths and seal the ends for you. If you need to do this yourself, wind thread around the rope on each side of the cutting point. Using small sharp scissors, cut through the rope one cord at a time. Seal the end immediately with a lighted match, which will melt the end together. This is best done outside.

Ruffles

Ruffles provide a final ornamental flourish to most home furnishings. They can dress up curtains, add depth to a curtain valance, give a finishing flounce to a floor-length tablecloth, and enhance cushion seams and tiebacks. Match up fabrics on a ruffle to the rest of the furnishing that you are making and include a contrasting piping in the joining seam. Or, use a contrasting color for the ruffle. Ruffle depth depends on the furnishing it is to be attached to, with larger items requiring deeper ruffles. Try out different ruffle sizes on a spare piece of fabric to see what looks best.

MATERIALS:
Light- to medium-weight furnishing fabric, matching thread
Plus for tiebacks: Heavyweight iron-on interfacing

FABRIC:
Ruffle depth: Between 2½ and 4 inches. Add seam and hem allowances. Measure all edges to which the ruffle will be added and double this for ruffle length.
For tiebacks: Draw Pattern B (see page 91) to the required size. You will need two pieces of fabric this size (or one of fabric and one of lining) and one piece of interfacing.

MAKING A SINGLE RUFFLE

1 Remove the selvages from the ruffle fabric. On the wrong side of the fabric, mark lines across the width with tailor's chalk to the chosen ruffle depth. Do this until you have enough strips to make up the full ruffle length. Cut out strips.

2 Join the strips using narrow French seams (see page 81) to make up the length required. Press under a ¼-inch hem twice at each short end. Or, if the ruffle is continuous, use a French seam to join one end to the other.

3 Press under a ¼-inch hem twice along one long edge, then stitch in place. Rather than hem the edge, use a machine satin-stitch (see page 80) to cover the raw edge. Or, bind the edge with a contrasting bias binding.

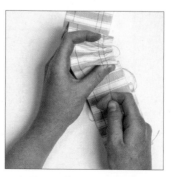

4 Using the longest stitch on the machine, run two rows of stitching along the raw edge. Stitch in lengths of about 24 inches. Backstitch at one end to secure and leave long threads for pulling up the gathers at the other. Pull up the gathers evenly to fit the required length. Wind threads around pins to hold. Tack the ruffle in position to the main fabric with raw edges matching. Stitch and trim raw edges.

RUFFLED TIEBACK

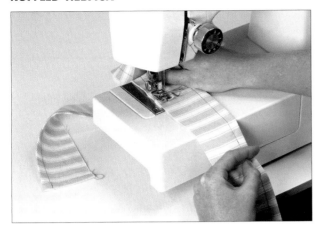

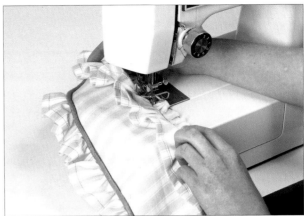

1 Cut out a curved tieback using Pattern B on page 91 and assemble (see Step 1, Piped Tieback, page 19). Cut out and stitch a ruffle length to go around the edge of the tieback following steps 1–3, Making a Single Ruffle.

2 Attach piping, if required (see Step 2, Piped Tieback, page 19). Then, with right sides facing, match the raw edges of the tieback and ruffle and pin together. Baste, then stitch. Slip-stitch the tieback back in place to cover raw edges.

MAKING A DOUBLE RUFFLE

Calculate the length required in the same way as for a single ruffle, but allow twice the depth plus 1 inch for ½-inch seam allowances. Join strips of fabric with open seams to make up the full length. Fold the strip in half lengthwise with right sides facing and stitch across the short ends or join to the opposite end for a continuous ruffle. Turn right side out and refold lengthwise. Press. Stitch rows of gathering threads through both layers along the raw edge (see Step 4, Making a Single Ruffle) and pull up threads. Tack ruffle to the main fabric, stitch, then trim the raw edges.

Braids

Padded, braided tubes of fabric form a bold, decorative strip that can be used to create stunning effects. Put several to work as curtain tiebacks. Or, use one to edge a floor-length tablecloth, border a plain bedspread, or outline curtain hems that sweep the floor.

Braids are most striking if fabric of different patterns, colors, or shades is used for each tube. To enhance patterned fabric, make a braid from plain fabric, picking out colors that are used in the main design.

For a coordinated look, use the patterned fabric for one of the strips with plain colors for the other two or use fabrics from other furnishings in the room.

MATERIALS:
Medium-weight furnishing fabric, high-loft batting, matching threads
Plus for tiebacks: Two curtain rings

FABRIC:
For a braid: Measure the finished length required. Cut each fabric strip 4 inches wide and the finished length plus one-third of the length to allow for take-up in the braiding. You will need three strips of fabric cut to these measurements plus three strips of batting 3 inches wide and 1 inch shorter than the fabric strips.
For tiebacks: Hold back the curtain and measure around it with a length of string to find the tieback length required. Follow the instructions above for braid strip sizes.

MAKING A BRAID

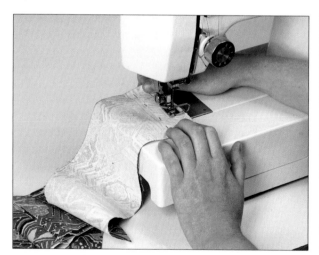

1 Cut out fabric strips. To join lengths for a longer braid, place one same-color strip on top of another strip, with right sides facing and all edges matching. Stitch across one short end ½ inch from the raw edge. Press seam open and continue in this way until you have the length required.

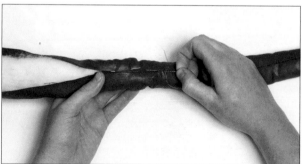

2 Press under ⅝ inch along one long edge on one fabric strip. Place the strip, wrong side up, with a thick batting strip positioned on top ½ inch from the short ends. Bring both long edges to the center. Pin the pressed edge over the long raw edge to form a tube with the batting sandwiched inside. Slip-stitch the pinned seam to hold it in place. Make the other two tubes in the same manner. Turn the short raw edge inside at one end of each tube and slip-stitch the opening closed.

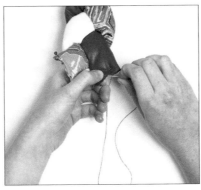

3 Overlap the three tubes at the finished ends. Pin and stitch them together. Temporarily hold this end firm by pinning it to an upholstered surface. Braid the three strips together, keeping the braiding neat and fairly loose. Make sure the long slip-stitched seams are at the back.

4 Continue braiding, measuring the braid as you work, until the required length is reached. Trim off excess, if necessary, allowing for a ½-inch seam allowance at the raw ends. Turn the raw ends inside and pin, then slip-stitch closed. Join the braid end strips together as before.

BRAIDED BORDERS

If the braid is to be used as a decorative edging, along a curtain hem for example, simply slip-stitch it in place along the finished hem edge.

Where braids join together, around a tablecloth or a bedspread for instance, only baste the braid ends closed (see steps 2 and 4). To attach braids to the furnishing, remove basting and, one at a time, slip-stitch a tube end to the opposite end of the same tube to form one continuous braid.

BRAIDED TIEBACK

1 Follow the instructions under Fabric, page 24, for cutting strips. Make a braid to the desired length for each curtain (see steps 1–4, page 24 and above).

2 Attach a curtain ring securely to the back edge of each tieback end and hang from fixed hooks at the required height.

Bows

The addition of bows enhances plain soft furnishings considerably. The easiest bows are tied from lengths of ribbon, cord, or a sash of fabric. For a larger, splashier bow, a stronger shape is created when the bow is made in three separate sections: loops, tails, and a wraparound knot.

MATERIALS:
Furnishing fabric, matching thread
Plus for tiebacks: Iron-on interfacing, two large curtain rings

FABRIC:
Make a bow from scrap fabric and use this to work out your measurements.
Loops: Measure length from end of one loop to end of opposite loop. Measure loop depth. Cut fabric twice the length by twice the depth and add seam allowances.
Tails: Measure from the tip of one tail, through the knot, to the tip of the other tail. You need two pieces this length by the established width, plus seam allowances.
Knot: Cut a rectangular piece of fabric the circumference of the knot by twice the width of the knot, plus seam allowances.
For tiebacks: Measure around the held-back curtain to calculate the length required. Cut a rectangle of fabric twice the chosen width by the length and add seam allowances. Cut a piece of iron-on interfacing to finished tieback size.

MAKING A BOW

1 Fold the loop rectangle in half lengthwise with right sides together. Pin, then stitch the long raw edges together. Press the seam open, turn right side out, and press again with the seam at the center back. Zigzag stitch across each end to secure.

2 Fold each end of the loop strip into the center, overlapping by 1 inch. Slip-stitch together to secure. Pleat up bow center by hand and wrap thread around the center to hold it in place.

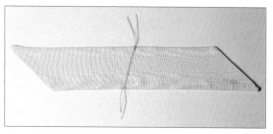

3 Place tail pieces together with right sides facing. Pin in place. To angle the ends, fold the lower left corner diagonally to meet top long edge. Press to mark angle. Unfold fabric and cut on pressed line. Fold top right corner diagonally to meet bottom edge. Press and cut as for other corner. Stitch tails together, leaving a 2-inch opening in the center of one long edge. Trim the points, turn right side out, and press. Slip-stitch the opening closed. Mark the center of the tail piece, then stitch two rows of gathering threads from one edge to the other at a slight angle, as shown here.

4 To make the knot piece, fold the rectangle of fabric in half lengthwise with the right sides together. Stitch the long edges together to form a tube. Press. Turn tube right side out, using a pencil to ease fabric through. Press seam to center back. Finish ends as for the loops.

5 To assemble the bow, pull up the gathers in the tail piece to match the knot width and secure the threads. Fold tail piece along the angled, gathered line, then position over the back of the loops and stitch through all thicknesses to secure. Wind the knot piece around the loops and tails to cover the gathers, overlapping the ends at the back. Trim if necessary, then fold under the seam allowance on the top edge and slip-stitch in place.

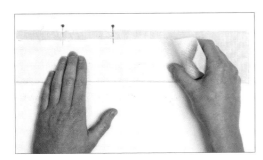

BOW-DECORATED TIEBACK

1 Fold tieback fabric in half lengthwise with right sides facing. Place interfacing on top, flush with folded edge, but with fabric seam allowance showing equally on the other three sides. Iron interfacing in place (see instructions on page 13). Stitch tieback along long raw edge. Turn right side out and press. Fold in raw edges at each end, insert a curtain ring in each seam, and slip-stitch the openings closed.

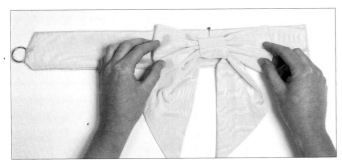

2 Make the bow as directed in steps 1–4, page 26 and above. The bow is positioned slightly off-center so it will appear on the front of the curtain. Fold tieback length crosswise to find the center, then mark a position about 3 inches to one side of the center. Stitch two rows of gathering threads across the tieback at this point, starting and stopping ½ inch from the top and bottom edge. On a pair of curtains, mark position for second bow on opposite side of center point. Pull up and secure gathering threads to depth of bow knot. Stitch back of knot to tieback.

Tassels

Tassels are fun to make, require a minimum of sewing, and provide a sumptuous finish on everything from cushions and window treatments to bedcovers, wall hangings, and even tiebacks.

Knitting cotton or wool, embroidery thread, and string all are suitable for making tassels.

MATERIALS:
Two colors of double-knitting cotton yarn, 1½-inch-diameter plastic-foam ball, tapestry needle, 6×6½-inch cardboard rectangle, small two-hole button
Plus for tieback: ⅝-inch-diameter tube (plastic or cardboard), small two-hole button

MAKING A TASSEL

1 Make a hole through the center of the plastic-foam ball. Start this off with the end of small, pointed scissors, pulling out the foam from the center until the hole is about ⅝ inch wide all the way through.

2 Thread the needle with as long a length of knitting cotton as you can manage (about 5 yards) and knot ends together. Take this through the center of the hole, leaving a tail hanging. Wrap thread around the outside of the ball and up through the hole. Place the strands of cotton in pairs, leaving a small space between each pair, until the ball is covered with 25 pairs of equally spaced strands. Secure the cotton through the center and cut off the thread.

3 Thread the needle with a length of the second color of cotton, securing the knotted end neatly inside the central hole. Working around the ball, weave the yarn over and under each pair of vertical strands. Continue weaving the second color until the ball is covered with alternating strands of yarn. Set ball aside.

4 For the tail, work with both colors at once and wind cotton around the cardboard length about 40 times. Thread a 12-inch length of yarn under all the loops at one edge. Slip the loops off the cardboard and tie the cotton tightly. Pass the thread ends through the holes in the button and knot to secure. Cut the loops at the bottom and trim evenly.

5 To make the cord, cut three 41-inch strands of cotton yarn. Holding the strands together, fold them in half over one finger. Twist the strands at the opposite end until they are tightly twisted around each other. Bring the loose ends through the fold and hold, letting the yarn twist on itself to form a cord. Stitch the loose ends together to secure them. Leave the needle on the thread.

6 Attach the sections by stitching the two ends of the cord together to form a loop (see photo, Step 5), then thread the yarn through the center of the ball and through the center of the tassel tail into the holes in the button. Bring the thread back through again, securing it to the end of the loop. Wind a threaded length of yarn around the top of the tassel tail and under the ball to neaten it. Secure yarn.

TASSEL TIEBACK

1 Make the tassel by following steps 1–5, Making a Tassel, but do not attach sections together.

2 For a 28½-inch, double-looped tieback, cut six 8-yard lengths of yarn (to avoid cut ends, measure out lengths, folding them back at each end). Holding the lengths together, fold them in half. Secure the loop around a doorknob; twist ends together. When the strands start to wind around themselves, bring the loose ends up through the loop and hold, letting the strands twist together. Secure the loose ends with thread. Wind yarn over the ends to neaten.

3 Cut a 1-inch length of tube. Sand ends, if necessary. Cover tube with pairs of yarn strands (see steps 2 and 3, Making a Tassel). To assemble the tieback, fold the cord so the ends meet in the center. Butt ends and stitch together. Push the cord through the covered tube until tube lies in the middle of the cord, covering the join. Using the needle, thread the narrow cord, which will be attached to the tassel, through the tube. Assemble the tassel sections (see Step 6, Making a Tassel).

Tablecloths and Place Mats

The addition of a new tablecloth or place mat dramatically transforms a worn or unattractive table. A basic cloth for everyday use is quick to make and easily enhanced with the addition of decorative trimmings or shaped edges.

Place mats are a good alternative to tablecloths, especially if you want to show off a handsome table. They can be made from fabrics that complement your furnishings. Mats made from vinyl-coated plastic fabric, which can be wiped clean, are both fun and immensely practical for small children.

A floor-length tablecloth on a rectangular or round table looks stunning and is a great way to disguise an inexpensive piece of furniture, making it into something special.

Style choices and measuring

Tablecloths need not be consigned merely to practical, protective use over dining or kitchen tables. Other tables in halls, living rooms, and bedrooms can be dramatically transformed by a cloth or floor-length cover. These can be as simple or as decorative as you desire. Choose the most appropriate skirt length, then add decoration with a ruffle (see pages 22 and 23) or add a braided edge to a full-length cloth (see pages 24 and 25) to highlight and stiffen the hem.

ALTERNATIVE SKIRT LENGTHS

▲ A short cloth is best for everyday mealtimes.

◄ For stronger impact, make a cloth that drops to a length halfway between the table surface and the floor.

▲ A full-length cloth is often the most decorative choice for a display table. It may reach to the floor level, or you can make it slightly longer so that it drapes over the floor covering.

MEASURING A TABLE

To measure the best length for a short cloth used at mealtimes, sit at the table. Measure the drop from table edge to just above your lap.

Square table

Measure the top from the edge on one side to the opposite edge. Add to this measurement the length of the required overhang and double it. This is the size of your finished cloth. Add seam allowances and hems.

Rectangular table

Measure the length of the table top from edge to opposite edge. Measure the width of the tabletop from edge to opposite edge. Add to each measurement the length of the required overhang and double it. This is the size of your finished cloth. Add seam allowances and hems.

A: Tabletop length   **C:** Table drop
B: Tabletop width   **D:** Overhang

Oval table

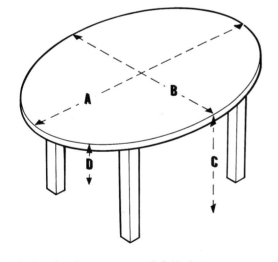

A: Tabletop length   **C:** Table drop
B: Tabletop width   **D:** Overhang

Measure the length of the table from edge to edge at the longest point. Measure the width of the table in the same way. Add to each measurement the length of the required overhang and double it. Add seam allowances and hems. This is the size of the rectangle from which the oval cloth is cut.

Round table

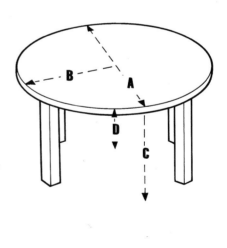

A: Diameter   **C:** Table drop
B: Radius   **D:** Overhang

Measure the diameter of the tabletop from the edge on one side to the edge on the opposite side. Add to this measurement the length of the required overhang and double it. Add seam allowances and hems. This is the size of the square from which the circular cloth is cut.

Bordered square cloth ✂

These two projects show how borders enliven a basic square cloth. The first uses strips of fabric to create a square "frame," which is then stitched to the main cloth. The second shows how to make a zigzag border to hang from a fitted cloth. When adding a border, use fabric of the same weight and fiber content as the material for the cloth itself.

It is possible that you will have to join fabric widths to make a square of fabric the right size. If this is the case, allow for a full fabric width in the center of the table and add narrower panels of equal width on each side. This avoids having a seam down the middle of the cloth.

Coordinating napkins can be made quickly and easily from either the same fabric as the cloth or from the border fabric.

MATERIALS:
Easy-care furnishing fabric, matching thread, coordinating fabric of same weight, template material for pattern

FABRIC:
Measure table (pages 32 and 33) and determine cloth size. Add ½-inch hems.
For a border: Use the cloth size to determine lengths, and cut four lengths of your chosen border width, adding ½ inch all around. Add extra to the length if pattern matching is required.
For a zigzag border: Plan for eight lengths of border fabric; each should equal the tabletop length plus 1 inch; make the width 3½ inches wider than the depth of the zigzag shape (see step 1, page 35).

APPLIED BORDER

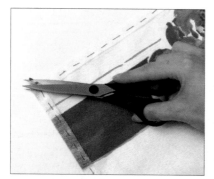

1 Cut out fabric to the required size, centering any bold design. Join widths with flat-fell seams (see page 81). Press a ½-inch single hem to the right side of the fabric along all sides; baste in place. Trim hem fabric on corners diagonally to lie flat.

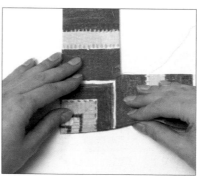

2 On inner long edge of border strips, press ½ inch to wrong side. Pin short edges of two strips together, right sides facing. Baste, then stitch on the diagonal to miter the corner (see page 83). Miter all corners; trim. Press under a ½-inch hem.

3 Place the border, right side up, over the right side of the main fabric, matching the outer edges of the cloth and the border. Pin, baste, then topstitch the border to the cloth, machine-stitching close to the inner and outer edges.

ZIGZAG BORDER

1 Cut the cloth to fit the tabletop exactly, plus the seam allowance. Decide on the width and depth of each zigzag (the zigzags should divide equally into each side of the cloth and finish with a complete shape at each end). On template material, draw a rectangle to these measurements, adding 2 inches to the length and 3½ inches to the width.

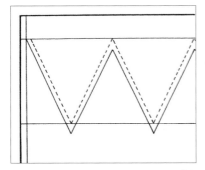

2 On the template rectangle, draw a vertical line 1 inch from each side. Draw a horizontal line ½ inch from the top (for the seam allowance), then draw a second horizontal line 1½ inches below this (for the top border). Starting 1 inch from one side, mark off widths for each zigzag on this second line. Mark the depth for the zigzags, then draw a third line across the template shape. Mark the tip of each zigzag on this line. Join marks with a dotted stitching line. Draw cutting lines ½ inch outside dotted lines and the top border sides.

3 Cut out the template. Use the template to cut eight border lengths. With right sides facing, baste pairs of border lengths together along the sides and the zigzag edges. Stitch, clip corners, turn right side out, and press. Press under a ½-inch hem all around the top opening and baste. Repeat for all border pieces.

4 To attach the border, cut out a ½-inch square in each corner of the cloth fabric. Or, make a ½-inch diagonal snip into each corner and press under excess on the straight grain to form a square, notched-out corner. Matching up border edges on each corner, encase the raw edge of the cloth in the basted border edge and baste through all layers. Stitch the border in place.

Child's place mat

Wipeable fabric, such as vinyl-coated plastic, is ideal to use for a child's place mat. This practical design, shaped as a grinning black-and-white cat, should tempt any small person to enjoy mealtimes. The front paws contain two convenient openings through which the fork and spoon handles can be slotted.

The details on the cat's white paws and muzzle are topstitched in black before the pieces are attached to the main shape. These shapes are positioned with glue rather than pins, which would mar the fabric, before being stitched in place.

MATERIALS:
Vinyl-coated plastic fabrics in black and white, matching threads, yellow adhesive tape, tailor's chalk, tracing paper for pattern, dressmaker's pencil, vinyl bonding adhesive, light-colored dressmaker's carbon paper, clear adhesive tape, talcum powder or tissue paper

FABRIC:
Main shape: 12×18-inch piece of black vinyl-coated plastic fabric
Features: 6×7-inch piece of white, vinyl-coated plastic fabric for muzzle, eyes, ear centers, and front paws; ¾×6-inch strip of yellow adhesive tape for collar and tag

MAKING THE PATTERN

Enlarge the cat shape (see page 90) by 200 percent on a photocopier, until it is about 10¼×15½ inches. From this pattern trace two copies. Shade in the areas of one color only on each pattern as follows: the main body, back paw, head, and tail on the first; and the muzzle, front paws, ear centers, and eyes on the second.

1 Cut out the main shape from the black vinyl-coated plastic. On the back of the pattern, draw over the tail and back paw lines with dressmaker's pencil. Place the pattern over the right side of the plastic and trace over the lines again to transfer them to the material. Machine-topstitch over these lines with black, stitching twice to give them more strength, if necessary.

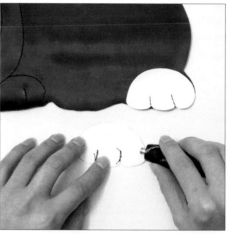

2 Transfer the paw shapes onto the white vinyl-coated plastic, as in Step 1, and machine-topstitch details in black. Cut out the paws. Mark a slot wide enough to receive a piece of flatware at the top edge of each paw. Apply the adhesive along the sides of the paws and stick down. When dry, topstitch in white, leaving slots at the top and bottom of the paws free.

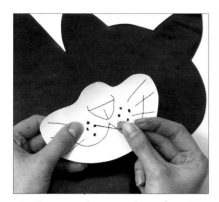  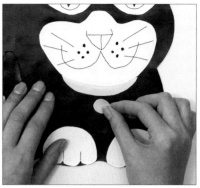

3 Cut out the muzzle and, using carbon paper behind the pattern, lightly mark in feature details on the white plastic (these can be removed with damp tissue paper). Topstitch the features in black, securing threads on the wrong side. Make round whisker marks with French knots (see page 80). Use vinyl bonding adhesive to stick the muzzle in place. When it is dry, topstitch in white thread close to the edge.

4 Cut out the ear center triangles, glue in place on the mat, then topstitch in white. For the eyes, transfer the eye shapes onto the white plastic. Glue a black plastic triangle in the center of each eye for the pupil. Use topstitching in black to define the irises and to stitch the pupils in place. Cut out the eyes and glue in position on the face. Outline main eye shape in white. Snip off long threads with scissors.

5 For the collar and tag, cut out the shapes from the yellow adhesive tape. Remove backing paper, if necessary, and position around the neck. This striking, wipe-clean place mat is now ready for use. For a personal touch, initials can be embroidered on the collar's tag with colored thread.

WORKING WITH VINYL-COATED PLASTIC

Affix shapes in position with glue or adhesive tape rather than pins, which mark the fabric. When stitching, use a ballpoint needle, a long stitch, and a roller foot, if you have one. If the fabric sticks to the foot when topstitching, dust it with talcum powder or stitch through tissue paper. Iron vinyl-coated plastic on the wrong side with a cool iron. Always test the iron on a scrap of the fabric before starting.

Quilted place mat

Using place mats allows you to show off the surface of a lovely table. Here, a fabric with a distinct motif has been chosen and areas of the design have been accented with quilting. The batting used for the quilting also provides some protection to the table surface below.

A second fabric is used to bind the edge of the mats. This fabric also is used for napkins, which have an appliqué corner design taken from the mat fabric.

MATERIALS:

Medium-weight furnishing fabric, medium-loft batting, matching threads, paper for pattern

FABRIC:

Place mats: For four 14×22-inch oval mats, you will need 2 yards of 45-inch-wide fabric. Allow extra for centering a bold motif on the top side of each mat and for cut-out motifs for the napkins. You also will need four pieces of batting the same size as the mat.

Napkins: For four 18×18-inch hemmed napkins, you will need 1¼ yards of contrasting fabric, plus ⅔ yard for the bias binding strips around the mats.

1 Cut a paper rectangle the size of the finished place mat, allowing a little extra for the puffy batting. Fold the paper into quarters. To round the corners of the place mat, position a dinner plate over the corner that has no paper folds, as shown here. Draw the curve and cut out on the line. Open up the paper pattern.

2 Using the paper pattern, cut out two oval shapes from the fabric, adding ½ inch for seam allowances and making sure the main design is centered. Cut a matching shape from batting. Place the two fabric pieces together with wrong sides facing and the batting in between. Baste the layers together, starting in the center and working out to each curved corner.

3 Select an attractive motif from the fabric design to use as the basis for the quilting pattern. Using a large machine stitch, stitch around the outline of the shape. Or, machine-stitch in diagonal lines, spaced approximately 1 inch apart, across the place mat, working in opposing directions to create a simple diamond quilting pattern.

4 Use a piece of string and measure around the edge of the pattern. Add 1 inch to this measurement for joining. Cut 2-inch-wide bias strips for edging the mat (see page 18), joining them on the straight grain to make the required length. Press border binding strip in half lengthwise, wrong sides facing. Open out, then fold long raw edges into the center. Press folds.

5 Open out the binding strip and align one of its raw edges with the raw edge of the mat with right sides facing. Pin the binding around the mat edge, positioning the join along the lower edge. Baste, then stitch together. Turn binding to the other side of the mat, enclosing the raw edge. Baste, then slip-stitch the binding in place. To join the ends of the binding, see page 19.

COORDINATING NAPKINS
Cut out napkins from the binding fabric. Cut out and apply motifs from main fabric to one corner of each napkin fabric square, using double-sided iron-on interfacing. Satin-stitch in place (see page 80). Turn under a narrow hem twice on all sides of the napkin and stitch to finish.

Rectangular tablecloth

This floor-length cloth, which is designed to fit over a table's top and sides, is an ideal way to conceal an unattractive table.

Using the diagrams on page 33, measure the table and calculate fabric requirements. Use these measurements to make up a paper pattern for all the sections, clearly labeling each. Making paper pattern pieces enables you to center any motifs and ensures that the pattern will match across each of the sections when the cover is stitched up.

MATERIALS:

Closely woven furnishing fabric, contrasting fabric for pleats and bows, matching sewing threads

FABRIC:

To calculate fabric requirements, refer to diagrams, page 33.

Tabletop: One piece measuring A×B, plus ½-inch seam allowances all around

Table side panels: Two pieces measuring A×C, plus 1 inch for hem, plus ½ inch for seam allowances all around

Table end panels: Two pieces measuring B×C, plus 1 inch for hem, plus ½ inch for seam allowances all around

Corner pleats: Four pieces measuring C×28 inches

Bows: See fabric details, pages 26 and 27. Rectangles of fabric for bows shown here measure as follows: loops, 24×24 inches; tails, 24 inches by table drop, less 4 inches; knot, 6×4½ inches. Allow extra material to match up a design with bold motifs.

1 Using the measurements you have taken, make a paper pattern for each section. Arrange these on the straight grain of the fabric, centering the motifs. Check the pattern match, then cut out the pieces.

2 First make the skirt. With right sides together, pin and baste a corner pleat piece to one of the side panels, matching side edges. Stitch together with French seams (see page 81). In the same manner, attach another corner pleat to the opposite side of the same table side panel. Repeat for remaining table side panel and corner pleats. Alternately join assembled table side panels with the table end panels to form a ring.

3 To pleat the corners, bring the seam on one side of the pleat piece to meet the seam on the opposite side, right sides facing. Mark the center (fold) of the pleat at the top edge with a pin. Stitch down the seam line for 4 inches to hold the pleat top. Position this short pleat seam over the center point marked by the pin. Pin, baste, then stitch along the top seam line to hold the pleat in position. Repeat for all of the corner pleats.

4 Zigzag-stitch along the raw edges of the tabletop section and the top edge of the skirt. Place the right sides of the top and skirt pieces together, matching up pleat centers to each corner of the top section. Pin, baste, then stitch with a flat seam. Press the seam open. Trim the corners to lie flat. Place the cloth on the table. Turn under a ½-inch hem, then turn under a 1-inch hem or the drop you require. Pin, baste, and stitch the hem.

5 To make the bows, see pages 26 and 27. Or, decorate just one or two corner pleats with an arrangement of fabric flowers (see page 43). Position each bow or flower group over the top seam on the pleat and hand-stitch in place. Press, then place the cloth over the table.

FLARED CORNERS

As an alternative to box pleats at the corners of the tablecloth, make flared pleats.

Cut four triangular pieces 28 inches wide at the lower edge, tapering to a 1-inch-wide cutoff corner point at the top. Make each piece the length of the table drop, plus 1½ inches for the seam allowance. Curve the lower edge of each piece. Attach to the table side and end panels in the same manner as in Step 2. Join flared side seams for 4 inches as in Step 3 and join top to sides as in Step 4. Hem the skirt.

Lined circular cloth

A circular cloth is made from a square of fabric. For a small table, the initial square can be made from one piece of material. For a larger cloth, it will be necessary to join widths of fabric to make a square the required size. To avoid an unsightly seam down the center of the cloth, use the full width of fabric across the center and partial widths on either side. This ensures the seams occur near the edge of the tabletop or in the drop itself.

Use the diagrams on page 33 to calculate the size of fabric square needed, adding extra to the length if you want the cloth to drape over the floor.

MATERIALS:
Lightweight to medium-weight furnishing fabric, lightweight to medium-weight lining fabric, narrow Austrian cord shirring tape, matching threads, string, T-pin, pencil

FABRIC:
Add the distance across the tabletop to twice the distance from tabletop to floor. Make a square of fabric this size, adding seam allowances for joined pieces. Make a matching lining. Cut tape the cloth drop measurement plus 1 inch.

1 To join fabric widths, cut one full width of top fabric to the required length. Using the ladder stitch (see page 78), match the pattern and tack partial widths of fabric to each side to make up a square. Stitch the seams. Prepare the lining in the same way.

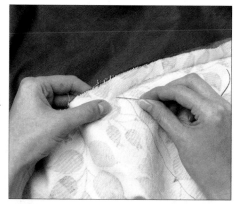

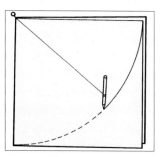

2 With the right sides together, fold the top fabric in quarters. Cut a piece of string a little longer than the desired radius of the cloth, plus ½ inch to allow for the hem seam. Make a knot at one end of the string and attach a marking pencil to the other end. Check the distance between the two to make sure it is correct, then attach the knotted end of the string to the center fold corner with a T-pin. Pull string taut and draw an arc from corner to corner as shown here. Cut along this line and open up the fabric.

3 Place the square of lining material flat, then place the top fabric over it, right sides facing. Pin to secure, then cut out the lining, using the top fabric as the pattern. Baste, then stitch together around the outer edge, leaving an 8-inch opening to turn the cloth right side out. Clip into the seam at approximately 3-inch intervals so the edge will lay flat. Turn the cloth right side out, press, then slip-stitch the opening closed.

4 To add a side flounce, as shown here, fold the cloth into quarters again with the lining on the outside. To locate where the table drop begins, measure from the center fold along one fold line a distance which is equal to the radius of the tabletop. Mark this point with a pin, then mark hem edge on the fold with a pin. The distance between the two is equal to the table drop. Open out fabric.

5 Remove the rings that come with the tape. Fold under ½ inch at each end of the tape, then position it between the two pins and baste it in place. Stitch the tape down each long side and across the bottom to secure gathering tapes at this point. Stitch across the top edge of the tape, leaving cord ends free for gathering up. Stitch two of the rings that come with the tape to each side of the tape top.

6 Pull up the tape to the required depth of gathers and secure the cords by winding through the rings in a figure eight. Place the cloth on the table and adjust gathers, if necessary. Stitch fabric flowers in place, if desired. Before laundering the cloth, loosen the gathered tape and remove the flowers.

FABRIC FLOWERS Cut out two shapes for each petal, adding seam allowances. With right sides facing, stitch around the curved edges, leaving an opening for turning at the straight edge. Clip curves. Turn right side out. Stuff with fiberfill. Turn under raw edges and slip-stitch opening closed. Topstitch petal lines. Make a center circle in the same way and trim with French knots (see page 80). Gather the inside edge of the petals so they curve. Attach petals to the back of the center circle.

Throws, Rugs, and Wall Hangings

Using a throw, casually or carefully arranged, over a chair or sofa is an easy way to give out-of-date, damaged, or mismatching upholstery a new lease on life—or a quick seasonal change.

Rugs can be used in much the same way to cover an unattractive or worn floor and provide a decorative focus for a room. Plain or patterned fabrics leftover from sewing projects easily can be transformed into an attractive rug.

Matching wall hangings, placed on each side of a door, fireplace, or window, create a festive touch at any time of the year. Or, choose a fabric with a simple, bold motif to make a wall hanging that doubles as a play mat for a baby's room.

Step-by-step instructions for making a selection of throws, rugs, and wall hangings are covered in this chapter.

Double-sided throw

A double-thick, double-sided throw adds a contemporary touch. It is versatile, as it can be changed from side to side to match your mood or a room scheme. A throw of this size has many uses—as a chair throw, a bed coverlet, even a picnic rug.

This throw uses two coordinating fabrics for a stunning effect. One square is cut larger than the other, and the extra fabric is folded around to the opposite side to create a border design. Decorative cording hides stitching on the reverse side and adds a neat finish.

Fine wools and similar woven fabrics, velvet, or chenille are all ideal for this design.

MATERIALS:

Soft wool or woven fabric in two coordinating colors, matching thread, decorative cording or braid

FABRIC:

Two squares of fabric: one square the size of the finished throw and the other 8 inches larger, plus braid for the border

The finished throw shown is 46×46 inches. For this you will need a 46-inch square of floral fabric and a 54-inch square of solid fabric. You also will need 4⅓ yards of decorative cording or braid.

1 Cut one square of fabric 46×46 inches for the bordered side and one piece of fabric 54×54 inches for the plain side. For the larger square, turn under a ½-inch hem to the wrong side and baste in place.

2 With wrong sides facing, center the smaller square on the larger one. Pin in place and check that the border is equal on all sides. Baste the two squares together, stitching close to the raw edges of the smaller square.

3 To make the border corners, fold the border around the edge of the top fabric and press in position. At the corners, pin the two side lengths together diagonally to create a miter (see page 83). Trim the fabric ½ inch outside the pin line at each corner. Turn the border so the wrong sides are facing. Baste and stitch the mitered edges together.

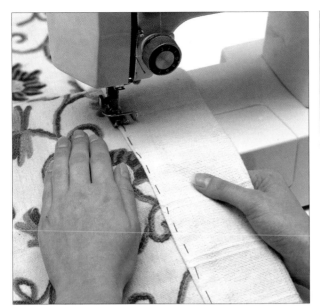

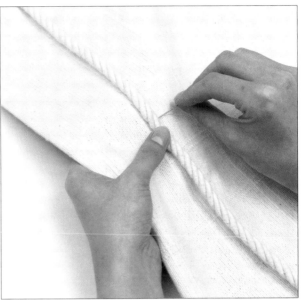

4 Reposition the border back to the right side, with the miter stitching inside. Baste, then topstitch the border in place. (For a neat finish, topstitch close to the fold on the basted hem.)

5 To add the braid, turn the throw so the reverse side is up and hide the stitching line by basting, then slip-stitching, a row of cord or braid (see pages 84 and 85) over the machine stitches.

FABRIC CHOICES

For the reverse side of the throw, choose a fabric similar in weight to the top fabric, making sure it can be cleaned in the same manner. Also, make sure any braid or trimming you use is preshrunk and that it can be cleaned in the same way as the main fabrics.

Plain fabrics are a good choice for the reverse side of a patterned throw, particularly if the color echoes one of those used in the patterned fabric.

Cover-up throw

An all-enveloping throw and easy wraparound cushion covers are a quick and simple alternative to making fitted covers for an old sofa. The covered cushions serve a practical purpose, helping to keep the throw in position. However, if you prefer not to cover the cushions, design the throw to go over them, securely tucking the throw into the sofa.

To measure the sofa, remove cushions and measure from the floor at the back to the floor at the front, following the sofa's curves. Add 4 inches for hems at front and back and allow 8 inches for tuck-in along the back of the seat. Measure from side to side in the same way, allowing for hems and tuck-in at either side of the seat.

MATERIALS:
Medium-weight furnishing fabric, matching threads, zippers

FABRIC:
Main cover: To calculate the length of fabric required, measure the sofa from front to back and from side to side. Work out how many widths of fabric you will need by dividing the fabric width measurement into the side-to-side measurement. Multiply the number of fabric widths by the front-to-back measurement.

Cushion covers: To calculate the length of fabric required for each cushion, measure around the top and bottom of the cushion from the center of the back gusset. To calculate the width required, measure from the center of one side gusset strip to the center of the opposite one. Add seam allowances to both measurements. You also will need a zipper for each cover that is 1 inch to 2 inches shorter than its width.

1 Mark and cut out the necessary number of fabric widths to make up the full throw width, matching up any design on the fabric across the widths. When joining widths of patterned fabric, place the widths side by side with the right side up, and baste together using ladder stitch (see page 78) to ensure an accurate pattern match across the seams. If using a plain fabric, simply baste seams together. Stitch with flat-fell seams (see page 81) and press.

2 Remove cushions and place the cover, wrong side up, over the sofa. Tuck in the throw at sofa sides and back, then mark the hem length, checking measurements at the center of each side and at the center front and back. Pin a double hem to this level. The corners still will drape. Stitch the hems, mitering the corners (see page 83). Press the throw.

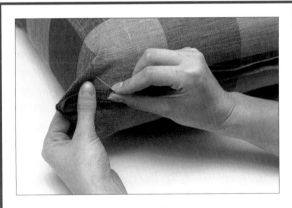

3 To check the effect, replace throw on sofa, right side up, and tuck in allowances, continuing the side tucks up and over back and down to front edges, and the horizontal back pleat over the arms. As an alternative to draped ends, pick up back and front corners and tie in a decorative knot at the center of each outer arm.

SIMPLE CUSHION COVERS

Cut out one piece of fabric for each cushion, following the measurements you have taken and matching any motifs to those on the main throw. Turn under a seam allowance along the short ends and insert a zipper in this seam (see page 87). Fold the fabric with the right sides facing and the zipper at the back edge. Stitch the two side seams. For neat corners, place the cover, wrong side out, over the cushion. Pin a miter across each corner (see page 83), then stitch. Turn right side out. Fit over cushion.

Braided rag rug

This rag rug is made from strips of fabric braided together. The continuous braid is then stitched to the adjoining length to form a thick rug. It is easy to match up a rug to a room's color scheme if you use fabric lengths left over from other soft furnishings in the room. However, to obtain an even result, it is important to use fabrics of the same weight.

The softly angled corners of the rug are created by braiding only two of the three strips at the corners. This makes the outside edge wider than the inside, forming a pleasing corner shape.

MATERIALS:
Medium-weight to heavyweight furnishing fabric in three colors, matching quilting thread, cardboard for template, pencil, yardstick

FABRIC:
The rug shown was made from 4-inch-wide fabric strips folded to 1⅝ inches wide. To estimate the fabric quantity, cut out three strips and braid up a sample length. Measure the finished braid length and use that measurement to calculate the number of strips and the quantity of fabric. To keep the folded strips even, cut a cardboard rectangle the same width as the unfolded strips.

1 Make a 4-inch-wide template from a piece of cardboard. Use this to mark strips across the fabric. Draw in parallel lines across the fabric, and cut out the strips. To avoid having the joins on each strip in the same place on the braid, vary the length of the first three strips you braid by about 4 inches.

HIDING RAW EDGES

The easiest way to keep raw edges from showing on the rug front is to press the edges to the back, Step 2. To conceal them on the rug back, tuck the center back raw edges in with your finger as you braid.

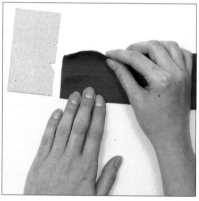

2 On the cardboard, mark one notch 1⅝ inches from one edge and a second notch ¾ inches beyond this. Using the template as a ruler, fold in one long raw edge of a strip 1⅝ inches, using the first notch for guidance. Press. Fold in the opposite edge ¾ inches, using the second notch in the cardboard for guidance. Repeat for all of the strips.

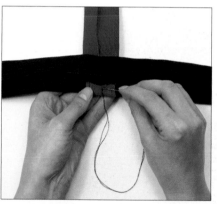

3 Unfold one end on each of two (green and blue) strips. With right sides facing, stitch together along the short raw edge. Press seam open, then refold joined strips as one long length. Lay out a third (red) strip, wrong side up. Place the long strip, wrong side up, over it to form a T-shape with the join at the center. Fold the end of the short strip to the back side of joined strips and secure.

4 Pin the joining point of the strips to a board and start to braid. In this case, green over red, blue over green, and finally red over blue. Do not braid tightly; allow strips to lie flat. To make braiding easier, roll up the separate lengths and secure each with an elastic band.

5 When the braid is 12 inches long, turn the corner. To do this, leave the inside strip on one side and fold the other two over each other twice. Twist the braid back on itself, press the outer strips in position on the corner with your fingers to neaten the shape, then continue braiding.

6 To stitch the braided strips together, use quilting thread and ladder stitch (see page 78). Do not pull the thread tight, but allow the braids to lie flat next to one another.

7 To join further strips, simply unfold the end of the strip, place a strip of the same color over the end of the first with right sides together. Stitch across the short edge ½ inch from the end, press the seam open, then refold the new length.

8 Continue braiding, turning corners and joining strips until the rug reaches the finished size you require. To finish off, trim each strip to a taper and stitch each taper in turn under a loop of the outside braid.

Child's play mat

The delightful design on this fabric has been used to full advantage for a child's play mat, which doubles as a wall hanging. Choose a fabric with simple, bold motifs that are easy to cut around.

The animal shapes on this fabric have been cut out and stuffed to form small toys. Attached with ribbon, some slip neatly into a matching animal pocket, while others are fixed in place with hook-and-loop fastening tape, making the mat a fascinating playtime diversion that provides a comfortable play area, too.

MATERIALS:

Closely woven cotton furnishing fabric, plain matching lining fabric, high-loft batting, narrow ribbon, hook-and-loop fastening tape, matching sewing threads, tailor's chalk or cloth marker, straightedge

FABRIC:

The finished play mat is 31½×47 inches. You will need two pieces of fabric (or one of fabric and one of lining) that measure 32½×48 inches and one piece of batting of the same size. You will need extra fabric, lining, and batting for animals and extra fabric rectangles for pockets. For each animal shape that slips into a pocket, you will need a 9-inch length of ribbon. For other animals, allow a piece of hook-and-loop fastening tape.

1 Following the sizes given above, cut two rectangles of fabric for the front and back of the mat and one same-size rectangle of batting. Use the tailor's chalk and the straightedge to mark the border line on all four sides of the rectangle, drawing it 4 inches from the outer stitching line.

2 Choose the shapes you want to use for the toys and cut them out, allowing an extra ½ inch all around for a seam allowance. For each toy that slips into a pocket, cut out a rectangle of the same design, allowing space for the toy to slip inside, plus seam allowance. Cut ribbon into 9-inch lengths, allowing one length for each pocket.

3 For each pocket, press under a ½-inch hem along the sides and bottom edge and baste in place. On the top edge, turn under a ½-inch hem twice and stitch. Pin pockets on the right side of the mat front, matching up the designs. Do not position pockets over the border line or too close to the center. Baste, then stitch pockets in place.

4 To make the stuffed animals, cut out one motif for each animal, allowing a ½-inch seam allowance all around. Do not try to follow the shape exactly, but allow extra fabric around detailed outlines. Place one motif, wrong side up, on the lining and cut out a matching shape. With the right sides together, stitch each motif and matching lining piece together, leaving a 2-inch opening along one edge. Clip the curves, press, and turn right side out. Using a round-ended object, push batting into the shape until well-padded. Place one end of a ribbon length inside the opening of each animal that will slip into a pocket and slip-stitch the opening closed. Omit the ribbon for animals attached with the fastening tape. Instead, stitch the top section of the fastening tape to the back of each of these animals.

6 To attach animals, turn under the opposite end of the ribbon attached to an animal and slip-stitch firmly inside the matching pocket. Decide on positions for other animal shapes and stitch the bottom section of the hook-and-loop fastening tape to each position on the mat. Do not leave a baby unattended on this mat.

5 To make the play mat, place the play mat front and back together with right sides facing. Baste the batting rectangle over the top, then stitch around the edge, leaving an 8-inch opening along one side. Remove the basting, press the mat, and trim the batting. Clip the corners, turn right side out, and slip-stitch the opening closed. Baste along the drawn border line through all thicknesses, then topstitch through all layers. Remove the basting threads.

HANGING THE MAT

To hang the mat, attach loops along the top edge and slip through a pole attached to the wall at play height. Do not use as a quilt.

Quilted wall hanging ✂

This hanging uses large and small motifs cut from a fabric panel. Each shape is backed by a mirror image from the design and sandwiched with batting. The motifs are arranged down strips of ribbon to complete the design. The large motifs are stitched around the ribbon, rather than attached to it, while the small motifs are tacked in place. If the fabric you choose does not include mirror images of the motifs, or if it is particularly expensive, back the shapes with plain lining fabric.

MATERIALS:
Furnishing fabric with bold motifs, lining fabric (if mirror-image motifs are not included in the design), low-loft batting, ribbon, matching sewing threads, glitter dimensional fabric paint

FABRIC:
You will need a piece of fabric that includes enough full motifs for each hanging motif, plus a mirror image of each. Or, buy enough fabric for single motifs and purchase lining for the backs. You also will need the same amount of batting as the fabric. For one hanging, you will need three pieces of 1⅝-inch-wide ribbon: two pieces the length of the hanging plus 1 inch (for ½-inch seam allowances); the third piece 16½ inches long (for a bow).

1 To create the basis for the hanging, cut two lengths of ribbon the length of the hanging plus 1 inch. Cut 2 inches from one of the lengths. Cut an inverted V-notch in each length at the bottom short end. Turn under a ½-inch hem twice across the top short end of each length and slip-stitch in place. Use the remaining length of ribbon to tie a bow for the top of the hanging. Cut notches in ends of bow.

2 Choose one large and one small motif from the design, using single elements as well as groups of motifs to make a single shape. Press the fabric, then cut out one example of each motif, allowing at

least ¾ inch around each motif. Do not try to follow a complicated outline exactly. With right sides together, pin a motif to its mirror image, carefully lining up the outlines. Cut out the second shape following the outline of the first. If you have no mirror images, cut out the second shape from lining fabric. Also, cut out one of each smaller shape from batting and two of each larger shape from batting. Repeat until you have cut out all the motifs required for the hanging.

3 To prepare small motifs, pin sets of shapes together, sandwiching the batting in between. Check that the back and front outlines match exactly and pin in position. Knot the end of a basting thread. Working from the center, baste out to each corner to secure the pieces. Use extra basting lines where necessary. Using a large, straight machine-stitch, stitch along lines in the design, such as leaf veins or flower-petal centers.

4 To stitch the small motifs, set your sewing machine for satin stitching and use thread to match the background color. Satin-stitch around the motif or set of motifs. Do not attempt to follow a complicated outline; instead, curve around the shapes. When you are finished stitching the motif, remove the basting threads. Cut through all layers close to the stitched outline.

5 Place the two lengths of ribbon side by side, right sides up, and spaced ¼ inch apart. Position the first large motif, with one batting shape behind it, over the ribbons near the top, and pin in position. Turn the hanging over and place a second batting shape and mirror image over the back, carefully matching up the outlines with those on the opposite side. Pin, then baste in position (see Step 3). Straight-stitch along any lines or curves in the design you want to stand out, then satin-stitch all layers together around the outside edge. Trim around the edges of the motif, being careful not to cut into the ribbon.

6 Stitch the remaining large motifs in the same manner, making sure there is enough space to attach small motifs between them. To complete the design, pin the small motifs in position and check the effect. When you are satisfied with the arrangement, the motifs either can be glued to the ribbon using fabric adhesive or stitched in place where appropriate, following leaf veins or flower-petal lines. Attach the bow at the top and hang using a large ring.

ADDING HIGHLIGHTS
To highlight the design, apply glitter dimensional fabric paint, following the manufacturer's instructions.

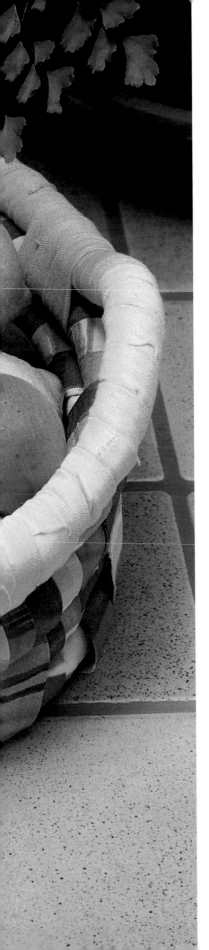

Storage and Screens

No matter what you have to hide—or house—you can use fabric to solve the problem. In this chapter, we show you how to:

• Create a fabric-covered coil basket that's ideal for kitchen, bedroom, bath, or sewing room.

• Make curtains and panels to decoratively hide the contents of a glass-fronted cupboard or an open clothes storage nook. Where narrow alcoves are used for storage, curtains can conceal the area and create a softly draped look for stark walls.

• Craft an artful, fabric-covered screen for concealing an unlit fireplace or to disguise other less-than-attractive areas in your home. Screens are particularly effective when they use a single, eye-catching motif.

Cupboard curtains

Glass-fronted cupboards may not always contain items that you wish to show off. If you prefer to hide the contents, give cupboards a whole new decorative finish with curtains fixed to the inside of the doors.

These curtains are made with a casing that takes a rod or stretched curtain wire at the top and bottom edges. To maintain the decorative look when the doors are opened, a ruffled edging is included. Before starting, make sure there is enough room to hang a curtain between the cupboard doors and interior shelves.

MATERIALS:
Lightweight to medium-weight furnishing fabric, matching thread, curtain wires or rods

FABRIC:
Attach the curtain rods or stretched wires out of sight (above, below, and outside the sides of the opening). To work out fabric quantities, measure the distance between the top and bottom rods. To this measurement, add twice the rod thickness plus ½ inch; also add 2 inches for 1-inch-deep ruffles and 1 inch for ½-inch seam allowances.

For the width, measure rod or stretched wire length and multiply by two or three times for the fabric width. (Transparent or fine fabrics such as voile, net, lace, and muslin look best gathered up to three times the width of the rod. For heavier materials, plan a width twice the length of the rod.) Add 2 inches for side hems.

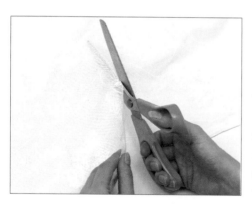

1 Cut out fabric to the required size. If you need to join fabric widths, use narrow French seams (see page 81) and match up any design across the widths.

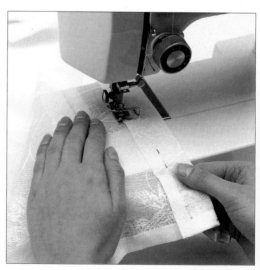

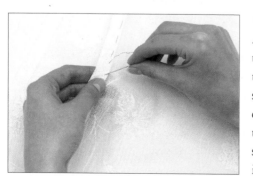

2 For the side hems, press under ½ inch twice along each side of the curtain. Baste, then machine-stitch the hems in place.

3 Press under a ½-inch hem along the top edge of the curtain. Add 1¼ inches to the rod thickness (for the top casing and ruffle measurement) and fold over pressed edge to this depth. Pin, then stitch along the hem edge. Repeat for the bottom edge.

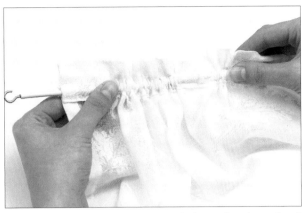

4 To make the rod casing, measure the rod thickness plus ¼ inch from the hem edge. Using tailor's chalk, draw a line at this depth, parallel to the hem edge. Pin the double thickness of fabric together. Baste, then stitch along the marked line. Press curtain. Repeat for bottom rod casing.

5 To hang the curtain, thread the rod or length of wire through each casing. Adjust the curtain gathers so that they are even along the length and hang the curtain in the cupboard.

SIMPLE FABRIC PANEL

A design that might get lost in the gathers of a curtain can be displayed virtually flat.

Measure the distance between the top and bottom rods and add twice the rod's diameter plus 1½ inches. Cut two pieces of fabric this depth, by the rod length plus 1 inch. With right sides facing, stitch the fabric pieces together along the top and bottom edges, using ½-inch seam allowances. Turn right side out and press. Press under the side edges ½ inch and slip-stitch closed, leaving space at the top and bottom edges to insert the rods. Stitch across the panel to form the rod casings. Slip the rods into the casings and hang the panel.

Fabric fire screen

A simple base of medium-density fiberboard, cut to size, can be covered with fabric to create an attractive, one-of-a-kind fire screen. Here, a fabric motif is cut out and appliquéd to a plain fabric background, then stretched over batting on the front of the screen. For best results with designs like this, choose a background fabric the same color as the background color used in the appliqué motif.

Determine the finished size of your screen and draw the pattern on a large rectangle of paper, curving the top corners if desired. Enlarge the foot pattern (see page 91) by 200 percent on a photocopier to make it full size. Using a scroll saw, cut out one screen and two foot pieces from the fiberboard.

MATERIALS:

Medium-weight furnishing fabric with a large motif, plain furnishing fabric, fusing-adhesive material, high-loft batting, matching threads, paper for pattern, medium-density fiberboard for screen and feet, paint, masking tape, glue, staple gun, air-soluble marker, handle, braid

FABRIC:

Motif: You will need a rectangle of patterned fabric featuring one complete motif with at least 2 inches of extra fabric around it and a rectangle of fusing-adhesive material ½ inch smaller than the fabric rectangle on all sides. *Screen:* You will need two rectangles of plain fabric the size of the screen plus 2 inches on all sides and enough batting and fusing-adhesive material to cover front of screen.

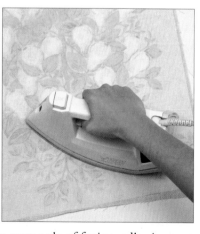

1 Press the patterned fabric, then cut out a rectangle around the motif to be used. Cut well outside the design, allowing a minimum of 2 inches around it. Cut a rectangle of fusing-adhesive material ½ inch smaller than the fabric rectangle on all sides. Center this, with the rough adhesive side down, over the back of the fabric. Press on a wool setting, allowing about 3 or 4 seconds contact so the adhesive on the paper is transferred to the fabric.

2 Cut around the motif, adding ½ inch around the design. Cut curves around any complicated outlines, rather than trying to follow them exactly. Using an air-soluble marker, mark the motif center at the top and bottom. Cut out one piece of plain background fabric to fit the size of the screen plus 2 inches on all sides. Fold this piece in half lengthwise, wrong sides facing, and mark centers at top and bottom. Remove backing paper from motif, line up marks on motif with those on the background, and press it in place.

3 To attach the motif to the background, use a close zigzag stitch on the machine and follow the curved outline around the motif. Stitch over the cut edge to avoid fraying.

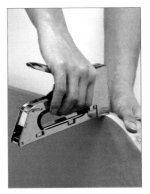

4 Use the screen pattern to cut out fabric for the back of the screen, adding 2 inches to all sides. Use the same pattern to cut out a piece of the fusing-adhesive material. Center the fusing-adhesive material, paper side up, over the back of the fabric. Press, following the manufacturer's instructions. Let cool. Remove the paper backing, then place fabric over the back of the screen, and press. Finish by stapling the fabric to the screen along all edges. Trim excess fabric.

5 Cover the front of the screen with batting, adhering it to the edges with masking tape. With the air-soluble marker, mark centers on the fiberboard and the fabric front piece at the top, bottom, and sides. Line up top and bottom marks of fabric and fiberboard and staple in place. Gently smooth fabric to the sides and staple at center edges. Continue stapling at 2-inch intervals, smoothing rather than stretching the fabric into place. Add additional staples, especially at the curved corners. Trim excess fabric.

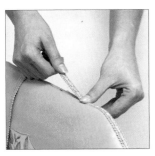

6 Glue a braid around the screen to cover the raw edges of the fabric. Turn under the braid edge at the starting and finishing points. Screw the handle in place. Paint the feet to match the screen background color, then attach them to the screen. Highlight the design with glitter dimensional fabric paint, if desired.

Narrow alcove storage ✄

In a room where space is at a premium, hang clothes from hooks across an alcove width and make a generous floor-length curtain to hide the paraphernalia. This curtain is quickly and easily made from two flat bedsheets sewn together to form a matching curtain and lining. To make the top ruffled edge, stitch a length of shirring tape parallel to the top edge, about 11 inches below it. The top decorative edge of the lining sheet is folded over to the front at this depth, creating an attractive valance.

MATERIALS:

Pole or rod and sidewall fixtures, clip-on curtain rings, flat sheets, 3-inch-wide Austrian cord shirring tape, thread, cord tidy

FABRIC:

Use two sheets per curtain and choose sheet size according to the width of the curtain you require. Single sheets make one 72-inch-wide curtain to fit a 52-inch-wide alcove.

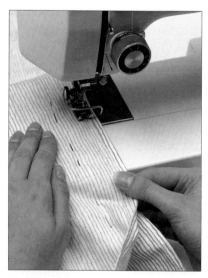

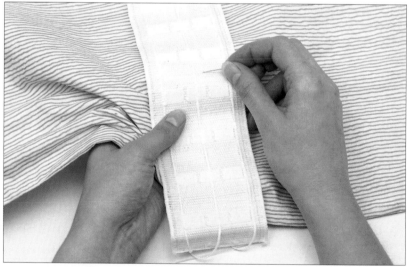

1 Place sheets together with right sides facing. Pin, then baste in place. Stitch together along both sides, using ½-inch seam allowances. Turn right side out and press.

2 Decide on the depth required for the valance. Using tailor's chalk, draw a line across the back of the curtain at this depth. Cut a length of shirring tape the width of the curtain plus 1 inch. Position the top edge of the tape on the chalk line, allowing ½ inch of tape to overlap at each side. Pin the tape in place. On the leading edge of the curtain, secure the tape cords to the back of the tape, then turn the overlap under and pin to the curtain. At the opposite end, pull the cords to the right side, ready for gathering, then turn the overlap under and pin in position. Baste the tape in place.

HANGING THE CURTAIN

Buy a pole to fit the width of the alcove, sidewall fixtures, and enough clip-on curtain rings to place them about every 6 inches along the curtain edge.

Measure the length of the curtain from the top edge of the shirring tape to the bottom edge of the curtain; position the pole at this height up from the floor or slightly lower if you want the curtain to drape on the floor. Attach the sidewall fixtures in place on the end walls with the notches to take the pole on the upper side.

To hang the pole, first thread on the clip-on curtain rings, then place the pole in the notches of the sidewall fixtures. Clip the curtain rings onto the curtain.

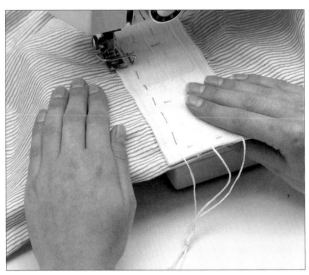

3 Stitch the tape along the top and bottom edges following the marked line on the tape, then stitch down each side. Stitch through the cords at the leading edge to secure them, but at the other end stitch beyond the cords. Pull up the cords to gather the curtain to the correct width. Tie and wind surplus cord onto a cord tidy. Fold over the ruffled valance edge to the front of the curtain and position the curtain rings at equally spaced intervals along the shirring tape.

INSTANT TIEBACK TRICKS

As alternatives to the tassel tieback shown, use a shell necklace and slip it over a cup hook screwed into the wall. Or tie wide ribbon into a giant bow, or roll embroidery threads together to form cord (see Tassel Tieback, pages 28 and 29).

Fabric-bound basket

Leftover fabric, cut into strips and wound around coils of rope, forms a softly shaped basket that can be made in a range of sizes and used to hold a variety of items from fruit to bathroom accessories or sewing supplies. Made from one length of rope, the basket is tough but malleable.

MATERIALS:
Furnishing fabrics, marine rope or ¾-inch-diameter cotton rope, large-eye tapestry needle, matching thread

FABRIC:
For a basket 13 inches in diameter and 3½ inches high, you will need twenty-five 1⅝-inch-wide strips cut the full width of the furnishing fabrics and about 7 yards of thick, fairly stiff rope.

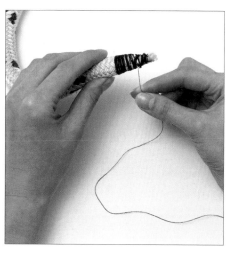

1 Using scissors, taper the end of the length of rope so that it comes to a point. Wrap thread around the cut end to secure. Starting about 4 inches from this end, begin to wind the first strip of fabric around the rope back toward the point.

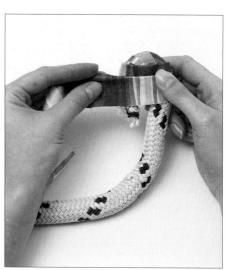

2 When you reach the pointed rope end, bend the point around to form a loop and tightly wrap the fabric around it to form the center coil. Continue wrapping the fabric strip around the rope, while spiraling the rope around the central coil.

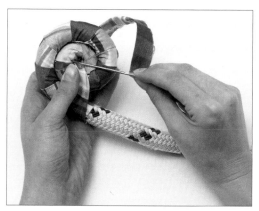

3 To lace the coils together, thread the strip end onto the tapestry needle and pass it through the central loop. On later coils, push it through the gap between the previous coil and the one before that. In this manner, lace every four or five wraps of the fabric strip.

AVOIDING FRAYED EDGES
To avoid frayed edges, fold under the left edge of the strip as you work. The right edge will be hidden under the next strip. After completing a lacing strip, tuck in any raw edges still showing with the outside edge of a pair of small scissors.

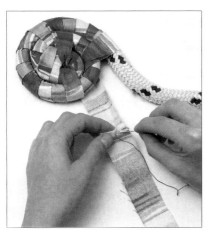

4 To attach a fabric strip when you reach the end of the first strip, place a second strip over the first with right sides facing. Stitch together across the end. Continue wrapping and coiling the rope as before.

5 When the base is the required size, start to make the sides by laying the next coil so that it overlaps the one before, lacing them together in this position. Continue forming the sides of the basket in this manner until the basket is the desired height.

6 To form handles, secure the top coil to the one before it; wrap fabric strips three times around the coil. Wrap the fabric around the rope about nine times and bend to form a handle shape. To attach other handle end, wrap strips three times around the coil below it.

7 To finish off, taper the end of the rope (see Step 1). Tightly wind fabric over the taper and the previous coil to secure; turn under the end of the fabric strip, and stitch in place inside the basket rim.

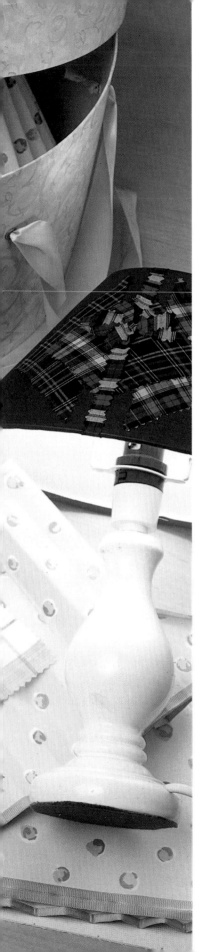

Lampshades

Lampshades can be quite easy and quick to make. Making your own shade considerably widens the choice of colors and patterns you have available and allows you to complement the furnishings in any room. With adhesives and stiffeners you can achieve impressive results, too.

Most lightweight or medium-weight furnishing fabrics are suitable, and cotton and linen are ideal.

If you don't want to start from scratch, you still can create your own tailor-made shade. Just add decorations to an existing lampshade, trimming it perfectly to your room's special scheme.

Choosing shades and bases

Table lamps form part of a room's decorative appeal and provide a light source that creates mood and atmosphere when used effectively. Depending on their shape and position, table lamps may create a background light while still lighting the whole room, or they may spread only enough light to enable you to perform close-at-hand tasks, such as writing, sewing, and reading. Small conical lampshades allow a spread of light, but need to be positioned high enough for the light to fall on the working area. An alternative choice is a shade hung low over a table on a long rod from the ceiling. A large shade works better in this situation.

BALANCING BASE AND SHADE

The color, shape, and material of the base and shade work together best when they complement one another. Before choosing a shade size and shape, look at complete shades and bases to see how they have been matched up and what effect you most like.

SHADE DECORATION

A plain shade looks pretty, but with the addition of a few carefully selected objects and trims, you can make it look fabulous. Fabric and clear adhesives let you attach unusual decorations to just about any lampshade you have in mind.

▲ This well-matched shade and base have a simple elegance that requires no further adornment.

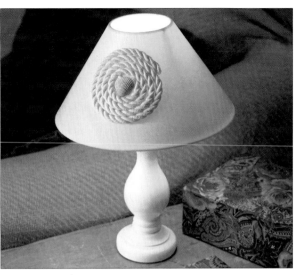

▲ Coiled rope and a seashell form a simple nautical design on this once-plain shade.

▲ When it comes to ideas for unusual geometric patterns, the combinations are endless. Triangles and rectangles of plaid fabric, cut with pinking shears, create a delightful patchworklike image on the front of this casual shade. Try overlapping a series of triangles around the bottom edge for a zigzag border.

▲ Ribbons let you tie up shades like festive packages. Fashion this jumbo bow with extra-long tails using wire-edged ribbon. Or, tie a ribbon into a neat bow around one side of the shade or lace metallic cord around the shade's edges through holes made with a hole punch. For safety, do not block the heat-escape hole at the top.

Conical shade

The sleek lines of a flared, conical shade add style to a room's decoration and act as an ideal basis for decorative trimmings. An inexpensive shade can be transformed with a new fabric covering and some extra decorative touches.

The fabric is fixed with spray adhesive to cover the old lampshade. Always follow the manufacturer's instructions when using spray adhesive. It should not be inhaled, so wear a mask and work in a well-ventilated area.

MATERIALS:

Conical shade, lightweight or medium-weight furnishing fabric, brown paper for pattern, double-sided adhesive tape, repositionable spray adhesive, fabric adhesive, ribbon for decoration

FABRIC:

Make a pattern from brown paper (see Step 1 below) and measure this for the quantity of fabric required. Align the center fold line on the paper pattern with the straight grain of the fabric. Measure at the widest point, then add a ¾-inch seam allowance on all sides.

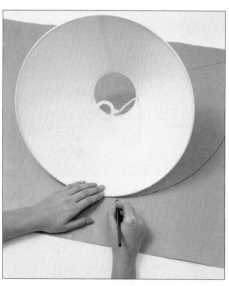

1 To make the pattern, draw a straight line on the brown paper, close to one long edge and at an angle. Lay the shade over this, matching the line on the paper to the seam on the shade. Carefully roll the shade on the paper, marking the top and bottom edges as you go. When you reach the seam again, stop and draw a second straight line between the top and bottom curved lines. Add a 2-inch seam allowance along one of the straight lines. Cut out the pattern piece, then lay it over the shade to check its accuracy. Adjust the pattern, if necessary, then fold it in half.

2 Place the fabric right side up and position the pattern on top by either placing the center fold line of the pattern through a central motif on the fabric or aligning it with the straight grain of the fabric. Pin in place, then cut out the fabric shape, adding a ¾-inch seam allowance along the curved top edge and the curved bottom edge.

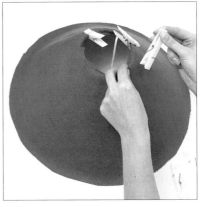

3 Fix a length of double-sided adhesive tape along the seam of the shade. Spray the shade all over with spray adhesive, then stick one edge of the fabric to the adhesive strip, making sure the seam allowances at the top and bottom are equal. Smooth fabric in place, keeping allowances even.

4 To attach the other end of the fabric to the shade, fix a length of double-sided adhesive tape to the fabric 1½ inches from the starting point. Peel off the protective strip on the tape, turn under an allowance of ½ inch on the raw fabric edge, and stick the fabric down on the tape.

5 Turn the raw edges on the top edge to the inside of the shade and fix in place with fabric adhesive. Snip into the fabric as necessary, so the raw edge lies flat on the wrong side. Hold in place with clothespins until the adhesive is dry. Repeat along the bottom edge.

6 To decorate the frame, cut four lengths of ribbon to fit around the shade from top to bottom, adding 24 inches to each length for bows. Position ribbons, evenly spaced, around the shade and tie in place with neat bows.

Pleated fabric shade

A pleated fabric shade fits neatly into most room schemes and can be made in a wide range of shapes and sizes. It can be created from a leftover length of fabric used for other soft furnishings in the room or from a fabric that will add color and sparkle to an otherwise spartan room scheme.

An added bonus is that this pleated shade does not require sewing skills. The fabric is fused to a heavy-duty iron-on interfacing, edged with self-adhesive ribbon, then pleated and fixed to the lampshade ring with strong thread and ribbon that is laced through holes to pull up the shade. The holes are produced with the aid of a standard hole or leather punch.

MATERIALS:
Furnishing fabric, lampshade ring with fitment, heavyweight iron-on interfacing, pencil, ruler, peel-and-stick ribbon (or ribbon and tacky glue), hole punch, narrow ribbon, tassel, fabric adhesive, bodkin, strong thread

FABRIC:
Measure the lower edge of the shade. You will need a rectangle of fabric twice this length by the chosen depth of the shade plus ¾ inch on all sides. Cut the interfacing to the length and chosen depth. For the edging, cut two pieces of peel-and-stick ribbon the same length as the fabric. For the narrow ribbon, measure the ring circumference at the top of the shade and double it.

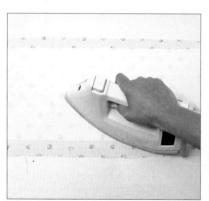

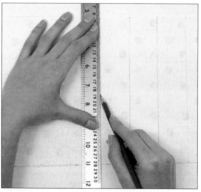

1 Cut out the fabric, making sure that the long edges follow the fabric design or straight grain. Place the interfacing centrally on the wrong side of the fabric rectangle and press to fuse it to the fabric (see pages 12 and 13). Once fused, trim off the excess fabric along the edges of the interfacing.

2 With the interfacing side up, make pencil marks at 1½-inch intervals along both long edges. Join the marks across the width with light pencil lines. Finally, measure ¾ inch from the top edge and draw a line along the length of the interfacing at this depth. This is the guideline for the punched holes.

3 Peel away a portion of the backing paper from one of the lengths of the peel-and-stick ribbon and, with the fabric edge on the center of the tape, gently press the ribbon onto the right side of the shade. Continue across the edge. Fold the other half of the ribbon to the wrong side and press. Repeat for remaining edge.

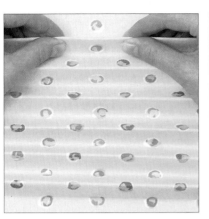

4 Working from the wrong side, crease the fabric along the first marked line. Fold up to meet the next line and crease in the same way, forming a ¾-inch-wide pleat between. Continue to fold and pleat until the end of the strip is reached. Turn the strip to the right side and firmly crease the pleats with your fingers.

5 Following the pencil guideline on the top edge, punch a hole halfway between each pleat. Pull up the shade with a strong piece of thread to roughly fit the lampshade ring. The pleats should fit comfortably around the ring. If the length is too long, shorten it. Remove the thread. Overlap and glue the strip ends together, making the join on an inside pleat.

6 To lace up the shade, thread a bodkin with the narrow ribbon. Starting at the center front of the shade (the side opposite the join), thread the ribbon through the holes and pull up to fit the ring. Knot the ribbon and trim the ends diagonally to prevent fraying.

7 Thread the bodkin with strong thread. Knot it to the ribbon on the inside of the shade. Pass the thread around the ring, then under the next section of ribbon. Continue until all of the shade is attached to the ring; tie off with a knot. Attach a tassel to the ribbon over the knot.

Tools and Techniques

This chapter covers the tools and techniques necessary to create great results time after time. Almost no extra tools are needed for the projects contained in this book, other than those found in most sewing kits, but using the right tools makes the job easier and the result more professional.

Here we explain tried-and-tested sewing techniques, showing you exactly how to tackle a particular task, whether it is attaching trimmings, sewing in a zipper, or creating a straight-sided corner or a neat curve. Information on securing raw edges, pressing your work, and clipping seams helps you to create a professional finish.

A final section on fabric care and cleaning methods has all the information necessary to help you keep the soft furnishings you create looking as good as when they were new.

Essential sewing kit

Good-quality tools not only last, they also make it easier to achieve consistently good results, so choose the best you can afford. A sewing box with compartments is a useful addition to a sewing kit, keeping everything separate and easy to find.

MEASURING AND MARKING

Tape measure: a vital part of any sewing kit. Choose a tape measure made of nylon or some other material that will not stretch and that has metal protective ends. Each side of the tape should start and finish at opposite ends so that you do not have to unwind the tape to find a starting point.

Yardstick: important for measuring lengths of fabric and for marking straight lines. Make sure that it is straight, has not warped, and that the markings appear on both sides.

Steel tape: the most reliable tool for measuring items such as furniture or windows when working out quantities of material required.

Dressmaker's carbon paper: useful for transferring designs or other markings from a pattern to fabric. It is used, like other carbon paper, with the shiny side facedown on the fabric and the pattern over it.

Tailor's chalk: comes in a range of colors, but white is the easiest to remove later. Always keep the edge sharp. You also can use a chalk pencil that has a brush for removing the marks.

Pencil: for copying patterns onto tracing paper. A soft pencil, such as a 2B, is the easiest to use.

CUTTING

Pinking shears: have a serrated blade which makes a zigzag cut. They are used to neaten raw edges, particularly on fabrics that fray easily.

Cutting scissors: should have a 6-inch blade and be flat on one side. Never use for any material except fabric.

Needlework scissors: are necessary for snipping threads, cutting into or notching seams, making buttonholes, and other close trimming jobs.

STITCHING

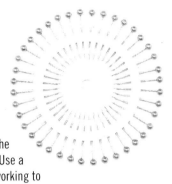

Pins: come in a wide range of lengths and thicknesses. Those with glass or plastic heads are the most visible and easiest to use. Use a pin cushion to store pins when working to avoid losing pins.

Sewing needles: keep an assortment of needles in your sewing kit. The most useful sizes range from 3 to 10. The higher the number, the finer the needle. Betweens are short, sharp needles that are ideal for fine hemming. Sharps, which are longer and allow more than one stitch on the needle at a time, are useful for tacking or gathering. There also is a wide range of specialist needles available, including a crewel needle with a long eye and a tapestry needle, which has an eye large enough to take narrow ribbon or fabric strips.

Threads: mercerized cotton is ideal for stitching cotton or linen. Choose all-purpose for general use and machine embroidery for finer fabrics. Core-spun thread, made from polyester with a coating of cotton, is tough and suitable for use on all but fine fabrics. Use silk thread on silk and wool fabrics. Buttonhole twist is the best choice for sewing on buttons.

Thimble: protects your fingertip when hand-sewing.

Needle threader: the flexible wire loop is pushed through the needle's eye, the thread inserted into the loop, and the loop and thread then pulled back through the eye of the needle.

MACHINE WORK

Sewing machine: basic machining skills and a sewing machine that does straight stitch, zigzag, buttonholes, and reverse are all that are needed to make the projects in this book.

Machine needles: are available in a range of sizes. Choose fine needles and fine threads when working with fine fabrics, thicker needles and thicker threads for thicker fabrics.

Machine feet: come in a range of designs for specific jobs. Apart from a standard foot, you will find a one-sided zipper or piping foot, which can be adjusted to right or left, a useful asset. A roller foot works well on shiny fabrics, like plastic laminated fabric, and a transparent foot helps you to see detailed work, such as appliqué, clearly.

Stitches and seams

Specific stitches and certain types of seams are ideal for use in different situations. This guide illustrates the principal hand-stitching techniques used in the book, and shows the different ways of joining pieces of fabric together.

PREPARING SEAMS AND HEMS

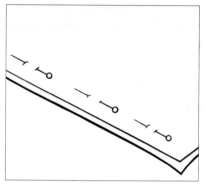

1 Pin fabrics together prior to basting. (On simple joins you can place pins at right angles to the seam and stitch without basting first.)

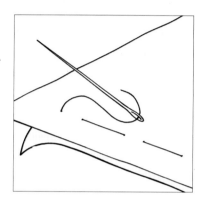

2 Baste adjacent to stitching line on the seam allowance. Use large running stitches that are quick to work and remove. Place permanent stitches on stitching line.

LADDER STITCH

This is the professional method used to tack two pieces of a patterned fabric together so that the pattern matches across the seam. It is done from the right side of the fabric. You also can use it as a permanent stitch if you take smaller stitches. Ladder stitch also joins the braids of the rag rug (see pages 50 and 51).

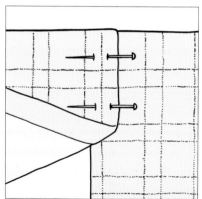

1 On one of the two pieces of fabric to be joined, press under ½ inch along the edge. Place this folded edge, with raw edges matching, over the second piece of fabric. Match pattern and pin in position.

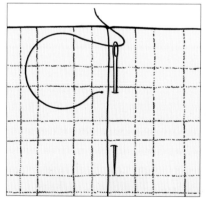

2 Fix the thread within the fold line, then take it straight across to the flat fabric and, running directly down the side of the fold, bring the needle out ½ to ¾ inch farther down the seam line next to the fold.

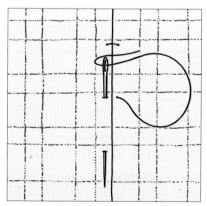

3 Take the needle straight across to the fold and push it down inside the fold edge for another ½ to ¾ inch. Repeat these two stitches for the length of the seam. Turn the fabric to the wrong side to stitch it.

HERRINGBONE STITCH

This is the stitch used to hold interlinings in place, but it also can be used to fix a raw-edged hem.

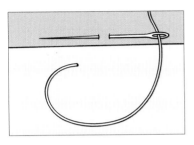

1 Pin the interlining to the wrong side of the fabric. Secure the thread under the interlining and bring the needle up through it. Working from left to right, take the thread diagonally to the main fabric and make a small backstitch, picking up only one or two threads of the main fabric.

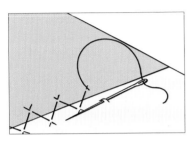

2 Still working diagonally, move across to the interlining and make another small backstitch through the interlining only. Continue in this way to the end and secure the thread in the interlining.

SLIP-STITCHING SEAMS

This is used to join two folded edges together. It is used when a gap is left in stitching to turn an item through from the wrong to the right side.

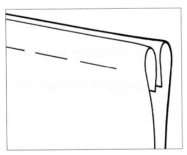

1 Fold under a narrow hem on both pieces of fabric to be joined. Baste to hold the folded edges together.

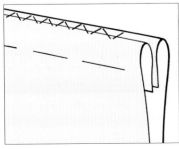

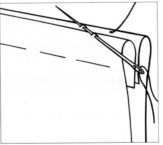

2 Hide the knotted end of the thread inside one hem. With folded edges held together, bring the needle into the inner side of the fold of the other hem and take a small stitch. Take a second small stitch farther along in the first hem and pull the thread.

3 Continue in this way until the opening is closed. Do not pull the thread too tight and ensure that stitches and thread are as invisible as possible.

SLIP-STITCHING HEMS

Although machine-stitching a hem is quicker, slip-stitching creates a neater finish as the stitches are almost invisible on the right side of the fabric.

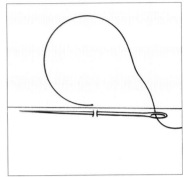

1 Fasten the thread with a knot or backstitch in the fabric of the hem, then bring the needle out on the folded edge of the hem. Pick up one thread, or at the most two, from the main fabric close to the hem edge.

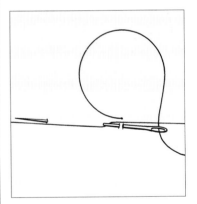

2 Take a long stitch of ¾ to 1 inch along the fold of the hem and pull the thread through. Continue in this way, picking up a thread from the main fabric and taking a long stitch along the hem edge, until you complete the hem.

FRENCH KNOTS

These small surface knots are used for the cat's muzzle on page 37. French knots often are used in decorative embroidery work.

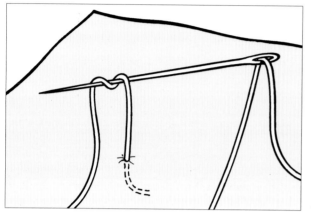

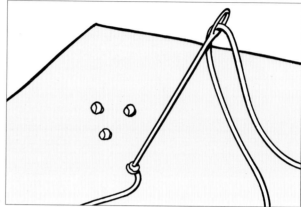

1 Bring thread from back to front. Pull taut with one hand while twisting the needle around the thread one or two times.

2 Reinsert the point of the needle back into the hole near where it emerged and pull the thread through to leave a knot on the front surface. Secure on the wrong side or proceed to the next stitch.

SATIN STITCH

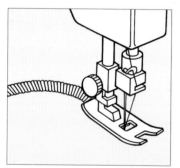

Satin stitch can be done on any swing-needle sewing machine. This uses a zigzag stitch set so that stitches are wide yet close together. It may appear as a buttonhole stitch on your machine. If not, set the zigzag on a wide measure with stitches close together and do a test, adjusting until you get the best effect.

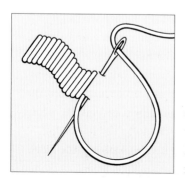

Satin stitch also can be done by hand, but this is much more time-consuming. Use long, straight stitches and place them close together side by side, keeping the thread flat and even.

GATHERING

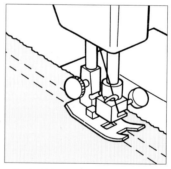

1 For gathering, use the longest straight stitch on your sewing machine. The length can be adjusted on your machine's stitch-length regulator. It is best to run two lines of stitching next to each other and about ¼ inch apart. When gathers are pulled up, the two lines of threads make the final stitching more even.

2 Pull up the two lines of threads and check that gathers are even along the length. Work long lengths in separate 24-inch sections. Secure pulled threads around a pin.

FLAT-FELL SEAM

The raw edge of a flat-fell seam is encased within the seam, but unlike a French seam, both lines of stitching appear on the surface. This makes it a sturdy seam that is ideal for use on items such as bedding or table linens that are regularly laundered. Here the stitching is done on the back of the fabric, but it also can be done on the front.

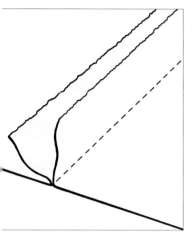

1 With right sides together, match up the raw edges of the fabric pieces. Pin, baste, then stitch ½ inch from the raw edges.

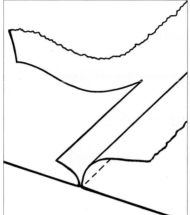

2 Press the seam allowance to one side. Then trim the seam allowance on the underside to a scant ¼ inch.

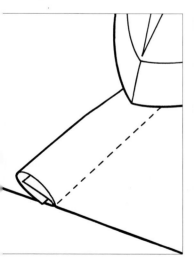

3 Press the wider seam allowance in half, encasing the narrower allowance. Press the seam allowance down onto the back of the fabric.

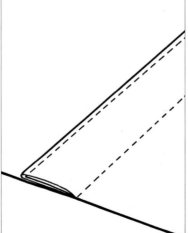

4 Pin the seam allowance in place and baste to hold it secure while you work. Machine-stitch close to the folded edge.

FRENCH SEAMS

A French seam is really two seams, one enclosed within the other. The raw edges are contained within the finished seam, giving a tough, nonfraying edge on the wrong side. It is a neat, narrow seam that is ideal for use on sheer fabrics.

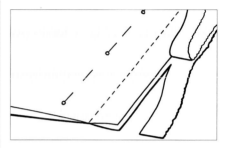

1 With wrong sides together, match raw edges of the pieces of fabric to be joined. Pin, then stitch ¼ inch outside the finished seam line. If necessary, trim close to the stitched line.

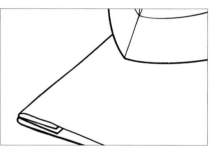

2 Press the seam flat. Turn with right sides of the fabric together and with the first seam line at the edge. Press well.

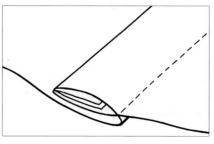

3 Baste, then stitch along the finished seam line. Press.

Curves and corners

Curves and corners need a little extra care and some special stitching and trimming if they are to wear well, look good, and lie flat.

When stitching a curve, work slowly to ensure the seam allowance remains even and use a shorter stitch than normal to give extra strength.

Mitering a corner neatens it and helps reduce fabric bulk. Mitered corners may be cut or, if the hem might be dropped at a later date, simply folded and stitched.

CURVES

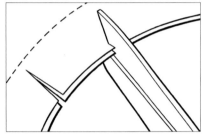

1 Clip the seam allowance at 1-inch intervals, cutting to within ⅛ inch of the stitching. Press the seam flat.

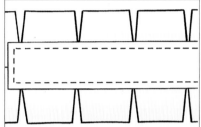

2 If part of the seam will get hard wear, strengthen it by stitching a length of narrow seam binding over the seam in this area.

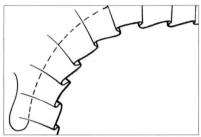

3 On a wide curved hem, use gathers to pull up the fabric evenly on the corner, then neaten the edge with bias binding.

STITCHING CORNERS

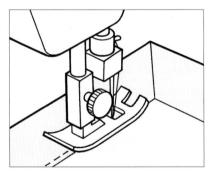

1 To get a sharp angle when stitching a corner, stop one stitch away from the corner and do the last stitch slowly, using the handwheel, if necessary. Leave the needle down in the fabric.

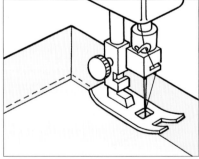

2 Raise the foot and turn the fabric, then lower the foot and continue stitching. To give the corner extra strength, use a shorter stitch just before and after the corner.

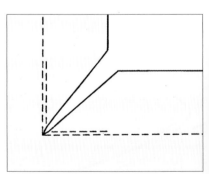

3 On an inside corner, run a second line of stitching just inside the seam allowance close to the first line for 1 inch on each side of the corner. Clip into the corner so it lies flat.

MITERING AN EVEN HEMMED CORNER

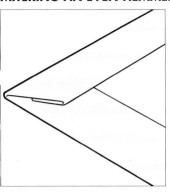

1 Press the fabric to the wrong side to make a single hem, then fold the fabric again to make a double hem. Press the folded edges well so that the lines of the hems are clear.

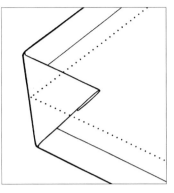

2 Open out the second fold only (the double hem). Fold the corner on a diagonal, matching the fold lines as shown. Press the diagonal fold, then open out all of the pressed edges.

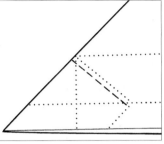

3 With right sides of the fabric facing, fold the fabric at the corner diagonally, aligning the diagonal fold lines. Baste ¼ inch outside this fold line, stopping at the first hem fold line.

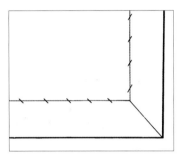

4 Stitch along the basted line, then trim the raw edge to ¼ inch, cutting across the corner. Press the seam flat, then turn the hem right side out, using a pair of round-ended scissors to push out the corner. Fold under the single hem and slipstitch in place.

MITERING AN UNEVEN HEMMED CORNER

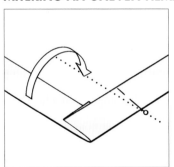

1 Press under a single hem as in Step 1 above. Press in double hem on what will be the narrower edge. Mark with a pin where hem edge meets lower pressed hem edge.

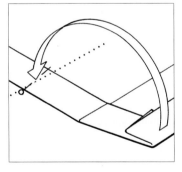

2 Open out, then repeat with the wider hem, marking the point where it meets the narrower hem edge.

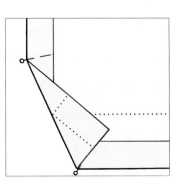

3 Unfold the second part of the hem only and, with single hems in position, press the corner fabric diagonally from one pin mark to the other.

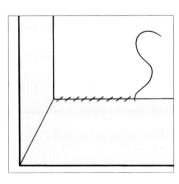

4 Either trim the corner fabric (see steps 3 and 4 above) or replace the double hems and slip-stitch the mitered corner without removing the corner fabric.

Attaching trimmings

Decorative trimmings may be applied to the edge of fabric or used to decorate its surface. Application methods vary according to the type of trimming and its position. Usually a trimming is added at the final stage, but some are designed to slot into a seam when it is being stitched.

Match the style, weight, and type of trimming to individual projects and ensure that all the elements can be laundered in the same way.

BRAID

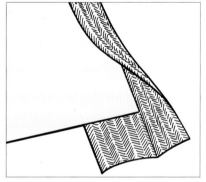

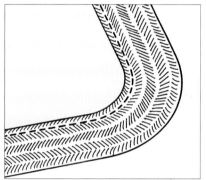

1 Apply fold-over braid with the narrower edge on the fabric's right side, basting both layers in place through the fabric.

2 Topstitch from the right side close to the edge. This also catches the slightly wider band of braid on the wrong side.

NARROW BRAID

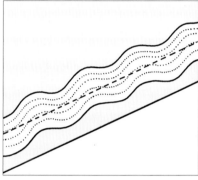

Narrow braid such as rickrack is attached with a single line of topstitching down the center.

FRINGE

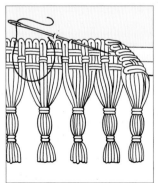

When applying a fringe to the edge of a tablecloth, throw, or bedcover, begin by turning a narrow hem to the right side of the fabric. Tack the fringe-braid edge in place over this hem and machine-stitch in position.

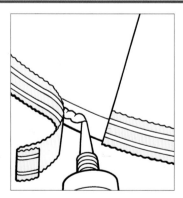

TRIMMING A LAMPSHADE

Apply fabric adhesive to the lampshade edge, following the manufacturer's instructions. Cut a piece of braid or fringe, allowing 1 inch more than the required length. Fold one raw end under ½ inch and, starting from the seam, glue the trimming in place around the shade edge. Finish at the far end by turning the raw edge under again to meet the first fold. Slip-stitch the folded ends together.

CORD

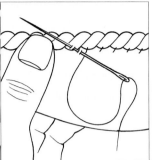

If the cord is not to be attached to the edge of the fabric, first mark the line it is to follow with tailor's chalk or a basting thread. Stitch cord in place using slip-stitches and a thread that matches the background fabric. Use your other hand to hold the cord in position as you work.

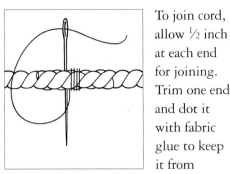

To join cord, allow ½ inch at each end for joining. Trim one end and dot it with fabric glue to keep it from fraying. Allow to dry. Trim the other end, apply a dot of glue to it, then press it to the first end. Let the glue dry and slip-stitch the new length in position. To disguise the join, wrap it with matching thread.

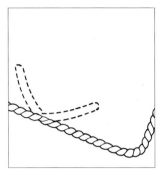

If the join meets over a seam, insert both cord ends in the seam. Close the seam and slip-stitch the cords together on the top edge to form a continuous line.

RIBBON

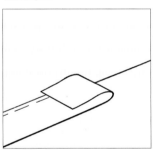

When applying ribbon, mark where it is to go with tailor's chalk or a line of basting. Tack the ribbon in place over the marked line. (When applying satin ribbon, which shows stitch marks, tack close to the edges.) To attach the ribbon, topstitch along each side using straight stitches. Or use zigzag stitches or a decorative embroidery stitch over the edges of the ribbon.

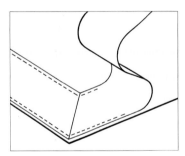

When applying ribbon along the edge of fabric, turn the hem on the fabric to the wrong side to the width of the ribbon. Line up the ribbon with the hem edge, mitering it at the corners, and machine-stitch in place along each side.

LACE

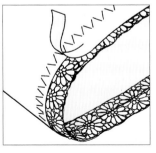

To apply a lace trim, place edging lace, right side up, over the right side of the fabric edge, allowing about ½ inch overlap. Stitch close to the lace edge, using a machine zigzag stitch. Turn to the wrong side and trim the fabric back to the stitching line, then go over the stitching line again using machine satin stitch.

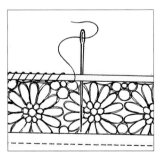

To create a lace insert, draw a line on the right side of the fabric where the lace is to go. Center the lace over the line, baste to secure, then topstitch in position close to each edge. Turn to the wrong side and cut away the fabric below the lace leaving ¼ inch along each edge. Roll these fabric edges to the stitching line and oversew to neaten.

Zippers and fastenings

Those items that need regular washing must have covers that can be removed easily. Openings can be unobtrusive, as when a zipper closes the gap, or obvious, as when bright-colored buttons and buttonholes are used to create a focal point in the design. Hook-and-loop fastening tape has many uses, not only for openings in cushions and covers, but also for attaching fabrics to hard surfaces for tiebacks, blinds, or a dressing table skirt. Below we show the methods used to attach a range of fastenings.

BUTTONS

Because buttons form a visible method of fastening, use them as a feature, choosing strong colors and designs.

Buttons usually come in one of two types. Most have holes in the button's surface for attaching the button, but some have a looped stem through which the thread slips. When attaching buttons, start by marking their positions with tailor's chalk. Use a strong thread and secure the end of the thread with backstitches over the mark.

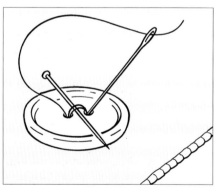

Secure a button with surface holes to the fabric through the holes, then place a pin under the thread and make about 10 stitches. Remove the pin, pull the button away from the fabric, and wind the thread around the stitches to create a short shank. Stitch into the shank and fabric, then knot.

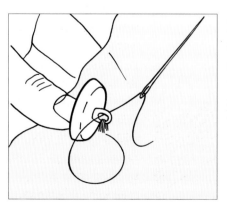

For a button with a looped stem, angle the button and make up to 10 stitches through the loop and the fabric, then knot.

MACHINED BUTTONHOLES

1 Match hole size with the buttons and mark the position for the buttonholes on the fabric with a fabric pencil or with a double sideways stitch at each end.

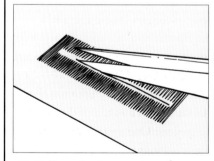

2 Follow the instructions for making a buttonhole in your sewing machine manual. To cut the buttonhole open, use a fine-bladed crafts knife. Place the buttonhole over a cork and start the cut with the blade in the center of the buttonhole. Finish it off with small, sharp-pointed scissors.

ZIPPERS

This is the best method of inserting a zipper in a cushion or cover seam, and the result is almost invisible. Insert the zipper before the cushion or cover is made.

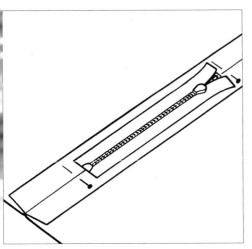

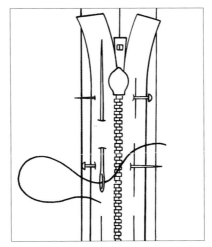

1 Baste the seam, then position the zipper centrally in the basted seam. (Where the seam remains open at one end and the zipper is to be positioned at the end, allow 1 inch beyond the end for a hook and eye or snaps.) Mark the position of the zipper with pins, allowing an opening ½ inch longer than the length of the zipper teeth, then stitch the seam at each end up to the pin marks and backstitch to secure the ends.

2 Press the seam open, including the basted area for the zipper. On the wrong side, place the zipper face down centrally over the basted area. Pin, then baste the zipper in position ¼ inch from the teeth down both sides and across the ends where the seam stitching ends.

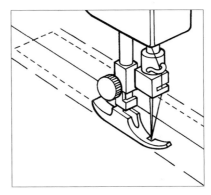

3 Insert a zipper foot in the machine, turn the fabric to the right side, and stitch just inside the basted line along both sides and across the ends. Secure threads. Remove basting and press, avoiding the zipper.

HOOK-AND-LOOP FASTENING TAPE

This comes in two sections, either as tape or in a range of different-size dots. One section has a mass of soft loops on the surface and the other has tiny hooks. Sections adhere to each other when pushed together. Hook-and-loop fastening tape, with a hook section that can be adhered to a hard surface, also is available. This type of fastening is ideal for valances and many types of window blinds.

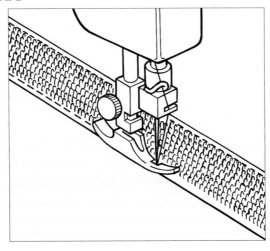

Place the hook section, right side up, on what will be the lower surface. Using a zipper foot on the machine, stitch in place along the edges. Slip-stitch the loop section, right side up, on the underside of the top surface. Hand-stitching will keep stitches from showing.

Finishing

Pressing after completing every stage of sewing helps ensure a professional finish. Have the iron and ironing board set up and ready for use while you sew, and if you do not have a steam iron, have a spray bottle on hand to dampen surfaces. Set the iron to the temperature recommended for the fabric and always test it on a scrap of fabric before you start pressing. When pressing from the right side, place a cloth over the fabric to avoid leaving a sheen. Use muslin or a similar lightweight fabric for fine fabrics and a linen tea towel, kept for this purpose, for other materials.

Neatening the edges of all seam allowances also helps to ensure a long-lasting finish, making the completed article as neat on the wrong side as on the right. There are several ways to secure raw edges, and the most suitable technique will depend on the weight and type of fabric used.

PRESSING SEAMS

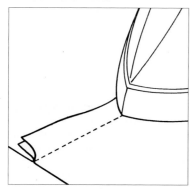

1 Press each seam as soon as you have sewn it. Press on the wrong side of the fabric, following the line of stitching. Hold down the iron briefly over one area, before lifting it and transferring it to the next.

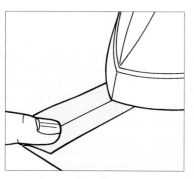

2 After pressing the closed seam, open the allowance and, sliding your fingers down the seam to open it with one hand, follow with the point of the iron to press the seam line open. Finally, press down the allowance at each side, using the full base of the iron.

PRESSING DELICATE FABRICS

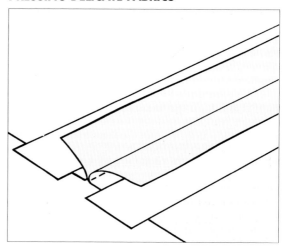

If pressing a seam is likely to leave marks on the right side of the fabric, cut thin strips of lightweight card stock and slip these under the seam allowances to protect the fabric, moving them down as you proceed. Fabrics with a deep pile, such as velvet, are crushed easily when pressed. Press them wrong side up, with a spare piece of fabric, pile side up, underneath. Use steam and a minimum of pressure.

NEATENING SEAMS

To prevent fraying raw edges, it is best to neaten the edges of all seam allowances. There are several ways to secure raw edges, and the most suitable technique will depend on the weight and type of fabric used.

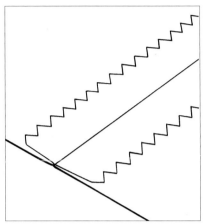

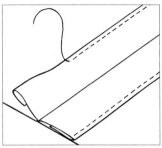

A straight-stitched folded edge is ideal for lightweight to medium-weight fabrics that are not bulky. Turn under allowance edges about ¼ inch and press. Straight-stitch along the folded edge either by hand or by machine.

Pinking is a quick, easy method that is suitable for cottons and fine fabrics that do not fray easily. Simply trim seam allowance edges with pinking shears.

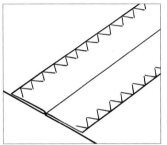

Zigzag edging is the most commonly used method of neatening raw edges and is good for bulky fabrics or those that fray. With a short, narrow, zigzag stitch, sew along the allowance, just inside the raw edge. Trim the edge just short of the stitches. On fabrics that fray badly, use a wider stitch.

FABRIC CARE

- Wash items before they become badly soiled and treat stains immediately.
- When removing a stain, never scrub it but, working from the edges, dab at it until the stain disappears. Scrubbing spreads the damage.
- On liquid stains, including wine, cover the area with salt to draw up as much liquid as possible. Place the item in cold water to soak for one-half to one hour. Finish by washing as you normally would.
- Tea and coffee stains should be soaked immediately in prewash laundry detergent, then washed as you normally would.
- On fruit and fruit-juice stains, rub fabric with salt before soaking in cold water. Rub with liquid detergent. Finish by washing in the usual way.
- On solids, scrape off as much as you can using a palette knife before treating the stain.
- On biological stains, such as blood or milk, soak fabric in prewash laundry detergent before washing.
- Iron tablecloths flat (do not press in folds) and refold in a different way after each washing to avoid well-defined crease lines.
- Press embroidery on the wrong side. Do not press lace cloths or mats; instead, lay out flat and pin in position, leaving until dry.
- If you are unsure if a fabric is colorfast, do a check on it before washing with other items. Dip a small, hidden area in warm water. Place this damp area between two white cloths and iron until the fabric is dry. If there is any color on the white cloths, the fabric is not colorfast, and the item should be washed separately.
- Sunlight fades fabrics, so avoid placing delicate fabrics close to windows.

CHILD'S PLACE MAT, page 36

1 square = ¾ inch

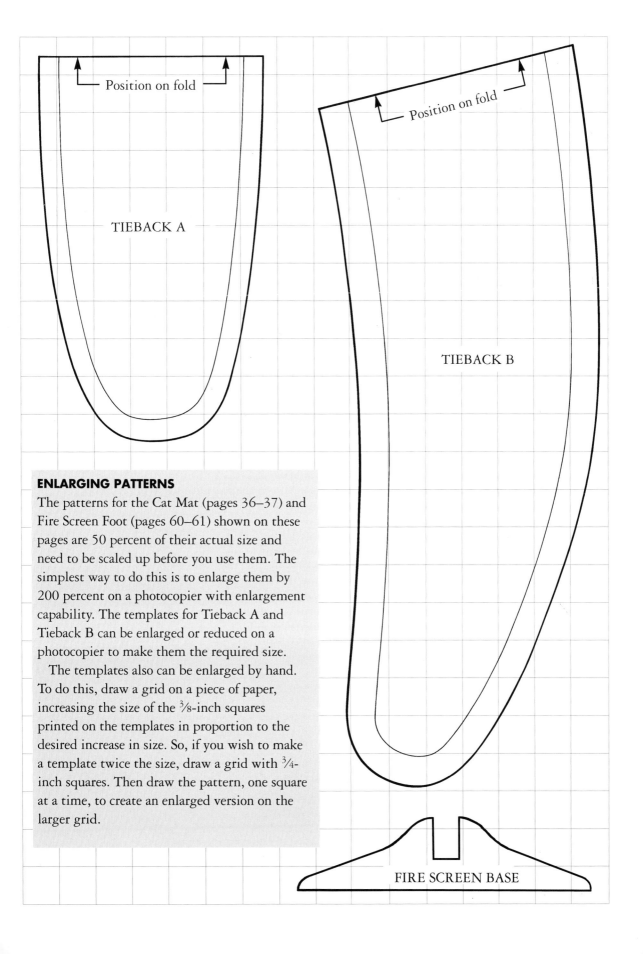

Position on fold

TIEBACK A

Position on fold

TIEBACK B

ENLARGING PATTERNS

The patterns for the Cat Mat (pages 36–37) and Fire Screen Foot (pages 60–61) shown on these pages are 50 percent of their actual size and need to be scaled up before you use them. The simplest way to do this is to enlarge them by 200 percent on a photocopier with enlargement capability. The templates for Tieback A and Tieback B can be enlarged or reduced on a photocopier to make them the required size.

The templates also can be enlarged by hand. To do this, draw a grid on a piece of paper, increasing the size of the ⅜-inch squares printed on the templates in proportion to the desired increase in size. So, if you wish to make a template twice the size, draw a grid with ¾-inch squares. Then draw the pattern, one square at a time, to create an enlarged version on the larger grid.

FIRE SCREEN BASE

Glossary

Appliqué
When one material, usually a cutout design, is laid over another and applied to it.

Basting
A temporary stitch to hold fabrics in position; acts as a guide for permanent stitching.

Bias
A line diagonal to the straight weft and warp threads of a fabric. Strips cut on the bias are used for piping and binding because they stretch and can be applied around a curve without puckering.

Bodkin
A large, flat needle with a blunt end and large eye, used for threading ribbon, cord, or elastic through narrow channels.

Double hem
When fabric is folded twice so that the raw edge is hidden within the hem.

Flat-fell seam
A sturdy seam in which the raw edge is encased within the seam and both lines of stitching appear on the surface. Ideal for use on furnishings that are laundered regularly.

French seam
A neat, narrow seam which is really two seams, one enclosed within the other. Ideal for use on sheer fabrics.

Grain
The direction in which the fibers run in a length of fabric.

Gusset
A section inserted to improve fit. For instance, in a box-shaped cushion the gussets are the four side sections that divide the front from the back of the cushion.

Interfacing
Special material, available in sew-in and iron-on forms, which is attached to the wrong side of the main fabric to provide stiffness, shape, and support.

Interlining
An extra layer of fabric, placed between the main fabric and lining, to add insulation, thickness, and weight.

Iron-on
The term used to describe the chemical reaction that occurs when one fabric (usually interfacing) is fused to another.

Ladder stitch
The professional method used to tack two pieces of a patterned fabric together so that the pattern matches across the seam.

Medium-density fiberboard
A man-made board that is extremely strong and will not break or splinter when cut. It comes in thicknesses from $\frac{5}{8}$ inch to $1\frac{1}{2}$ inches.

Miter
Used on a corner between two sides that meet at right angles, a miter makes a neat, angled "join" that eliminates surplus fabric.

Motif
The dominant element in a fabric design.

Piping
An attractive way to finish edges of a cushion. Piping is a folded strip of fabric that is inserted into a seam. It can be flat or form a covering for piping cord.

Quilting
The stitches used to decorate and hold two pieces of fabric together with padding in between.

Seam allowance
The area between the seam line and raw edge. The seam allowance needs to be neatened, especially on fabric that frays easily.

Seam line
The line designated for stitching the seam.

Selvage
A plain, narrow strip down the fabric sides that stops the fabric from fraying. Selvages should be removed before fabric is cut out.

Single hem
When fabric is folded once, either to the front or back, so that the raw edge is exposed. A single hem usually is used when the hem will be covered by another piece of fabric.

Slip-stitch
An almost invisible stitch used for securing hems or joining two folded edges on the right side of the fabric.

Straight grain
This follows the warp threads, which run down the length of the fabric parallel to the selvages.

Tension
The balance and tightness of the needle thread and bobbin thread on a sewing machine; the tension must be correct to create the perfect stitch.

Topstitch
A line of stitching on the right side of the fabric, often used as a decorative highlight.

Vinyl-coated plastic
A vinyl plastic, polyvinyl chloride, which is used to coat a fabric to give it a tough, wipeable finish.

Warp
Parallel threads running lengthways down woven fabric, interlacing with the weft threads.

Weft
Threads that run from side to side across woven fabric, interlacing with the warp threads.

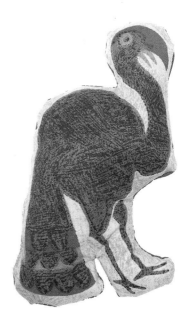

Index

Meredith® Press
An imprint of Meredith® Books

Do-It-Yourself Decorating
Step-by-Step Decorative Details
Editor: Vicki L. Ingham
Technical Editor: Laura H. Collins
Contributing Designer: Jeff Harrison
Copy Chief: Angela K. Renkoski
Electronic Production Coordinator: Paula Forest
Editorial and Design Assistants: Barbara A. Suk, Jennifer Norris, Karen Schirm
Production Director: Douglas M. Johnʳ ᵗ
Production Manager: Pam Kvⁱᵗ

A   g

DATE D

Editor in Chief: James D. Blume
Design Director: Matt Strelecki
Managing Editor: Gregory H. Kayko
Executive Editor, Shelter Books: Denise L. Caringer

Director, Sales & Marketing, Retail: Michael A. Peterson
Director, Sales & Marketing, Special Markets: Rita McMullen
Director, Sales & Marketing, Home & Garden Center Channel: Ray Wolf
Director, Operations: Valerie Wiese
Vice President, General Manager: Jamie L. Martin

Meredith Publishing Group
President, Publishing Group: Christopher M. Little
Vice President, Consumer Marketing & Development: Hal Oringer
Meredith Corporation
Chairman and Chief Executive Officer: William T. Kerr

Chairman of the Executive Committee: E.T. Meredith III

Cover photograph: George Wright
First published 1998 by Haynes Publishing
Sparkford, Nr Yeovil, Somerset BA22 7JJ, UK

All of us at Meredith® Books are dedicated to providing you with information and ideas you need to enhance your home. We welcome your comments and suggestions about this book on Decorative Details. Write to us at: Meredith® Books, Do-It-Yourself Editorial Department, RW–206, 1716 Locust St., Des Moines, IA 50309–3023.

© Haynes Publishing 1998. All rights reserved.
Distributed by Meredith Corporation, Des Moines, Iowa.
First American Edition. Printed in France.
Printing Number and Year: 5 4 3 2 1 02 01 00 99 98
Library of Congress Catalog Card Number: 97-71335
ISBN: 0-696-20731-1